FASHION DESIGN

Elizabeth Bye

Oxford • New York

English edition
First published in 2010 by
Berg

Editorial offices:
First Floor, Angel Court, 81 St Clements Street, Oxford OX4 1AW, UK
175 Fifth Avenue, New York, NY 10010, USA

Berg is the imprint of Oxford International Publishers Ltd.

Library of Congress Cataloging-in-Publication Data

A catalogue record for this book is available from the Library of Congress.

British Library Cataloguing-in-Publication Data

A catalogue record for this book is available from the British Library.

ISBN 978 1 84788 267 7 (Cloth)
978 1 84788 266 0 (Paper)

Typeset by Apex CoVantage, LLC, Madison, WI, USA

Printed in the UK by the MPG Books Group

www.bergpublishers.com

CONTENTS

ILLUSTRATIONS

Chapter 1

Chapter 2

Chapter 3

Chapter 4

Chapter 5

Chapter 6

Chapter 7

ACKNOWLEDGMENTS

I am grateful for the help of many individuals who supported this project. Kim Johnson, coeditor, made the original invitation and provided helpful comments and support. Alison Goodrum, coeditor, provided supportive observations, and Julia Hall, senior commissioning editor, was there to guide every step.

I am indebted to the many professors, colleagues in academia and the apparel industry, and students who have shared their experience and excitement with me. Special thanks to Heather Akou, Michael Alexin, Karen Bernthal, Janell Berté, Lisa Burdeski, Anna Carlson, Lucy Dunne, Sandra Evenson, Karen LaBat, Katherine Lauer, Yating Luo, Jessika Madison-Kennedy, Kathy McGee, Lyndsie Nash, Casandra Robnett, and Juanjuan Wu, who provided interviews that added depth to the text. I appreciate the help of my research assistant, Erin Jedlicka, for her organizational skills, attention to detail, and insight; of Eunice Haugen for her preparation of garments from the Goldstein Museum of Design; and of Dave Bowers for his photography. I am grateful for the support of Becky Yust, chair of the Department of Design, Housing and Apparel, as I tried to stay on top of everything.

Heartfelt thanks to my family and friends, who always seemed to know when to let me work and when I needed a distraction. This book is dedicated to Chuck, Elise, Elaine, and Tom. XO, M.

INTRODUCTION

Why study fashion design? The most common answer to that question is the desire to create beauty, pleasure, and meaning. Helping people feel good through the clothing they wear is an amazing opportunity. The magic of a new dress for a special event, a suit that helps someone feel confident during a job interview, or a uniform that protects an officer from danger goes beyond the stereotype of runway fashion. Fashion design is a dynamic, exciting field for those who make it their career and those who enjoy the final product. It is a field that involves both creative and technical skill and provides a service to society. Clothing is a basic need, just like food and shelter, and even the most basic garment needs to be designed. Fashion reflects current society as it evolves and changes according to world dynamics and the lifestyle preferences of consumers.

Fashion is meant to be worn; thus the human body and the clothing are the two most essential elements of fashion. The body provides the frame, the motion, and the inspiration for a garment, along with the desire, emotion, and intelligence to choose the garment to be worn. Clothing is made by forming a 2-D textile into a 3-D shape. It has a specific style and silhouette, size, color, and texture. It requires laundering, care, and storage and eventually must be discarded. When joined, the body and clothing can communicate and hold meaning, provide pleasure and protection, and be beautiful.

Fashion designers have the power to build and create, channel their imagination, solve problems, and have fun. Designers are agents of change (Pink, 2005) because, in response to their observations, they imagine things that don't exist yet. There is a great desire to develop new design ideas that address the consumer's aesthetic, physical, and emotional needs while supporting business, social, and environmental requirements. Stella McCartney expressed this in an interview with Suzy Menkes (2009, 3): "It's really the job of fashion designers now to turn things on their head in a different way, and not just try to turn a dress on its head every season. Try and ask questions about how you make that dress, where you make that dress, what materials you're using. I think that's far more interesting, actually." Change in fashion occurs as evolution, building the new based on what came before. Incremental changes can transform perceptions and actions, resulting in smarter design.

There is more to fashion design than the aesthetic component. It involves understanding the materials, the production, and the function of a garment, as well as the body and emotions of the person who will be wearing it. The care requirements of a garment and how it can be recycled or disposed of with minimal impact need to be considered at the beginning of the design process. There is a rush of opportunities and challenges in this field, and the need for strong designers is critical. Designers must be prepared to provide creative leadership to diverse teams that can address the complex future of the apparel industry. Experts in areas ranging from business to textiles and information technology to psychology can contribute valuable ideas.

Design economy

We are in an economy driven by design. Advances in technology and globalization have brought us products and services that function to improve our lives. In the twenty-first century, the products and services that are emotionally engaging, beautiful, and meaningful, in addition to being functional, are the ones that will succeed (Pink, 2005). Design must consider how the industry, the market, technology, and culture connect (Bonsiepe, 2007) and provide a way of thinking that makes it possible to imagine innovative solutions. Though fashion has always been known for its aesthetic components, it needs to develop a better balance with these other elements.

According to Faith Popcorn, trend analyst, reduced consumption is part of a new world order that will require the fashion industry to reinvent its strategies and priorities (Women's Wear Daily Staff, April 13, 2009). Consumers want value: good design and quality for a fair price. Creative products rather than a creative brand or image provide relevancy and a feeling of honesty and respect. Smaller, more streamlined businesses will emerge as companies focus on profitability and delivering a consistent message. Fashion for fashion's sake cannot exist when "ethics, the environment and the economy are all failing at the same time" (Popcorn, in Women's Wear Daily Staff, April 13, 2009, 8). Consumers will maintain their interest in fashion but only if the content of the product and companies has more substance.

Social responsibility and fashion design

Ethical, socially responsible practices are increasingly important to our society. The fashion industry is intimately involved with issues related to global labor and trade, sustainability, and consumerism. These issues impact quality of life in the short term and the long term for individuals worldwide. Designers and companies must act in ways that resonate with the consumer and society by balancing their ethical values with profit and conducting business in a manner that respects people and the environment (Dickson & Eckman, 2006). Practices across the industry, from fiber production and manufacturing to designing and purchasing, need to be evaluated to ensure equity for workers, healthier lives, and a more sustainable environment. A multitude of creative approaches can be designed.

This book presents a glimpse of the fashion world through the eyes of a designer with a conscientious perspective about the place of fashion in society. The first chapter on haute couture provides some history about the field and those who established the concept of fashion design. Chapters 2 and 3 describe how clothing is produced and the different roles that a designer can play in the process. Making connections to those who buy fashion is the focus in chapter 4. The stories of current designers who not only produce great fashion but also are leaders in our global communities are told in chapter 5. Chapter 6 looks at fashion design in a global context, and the book concludes with a look toward the future.

1

HISTORY OF COUTURE

The image created by the term *couture* has unequaled power. Luxury, elegance, and a refined mystique combine with the highest-quality fabrics, trims, and craftsmanship to offer a very exclusive group of women the experience of buying and wearing a couture garment. *Haute couture* directly translated from French means "high sewing." The real meaning of *couture* is much broader. Haute couture describes a select group of couturiers (historical term for designers) who are registered with the Chambre Syndicale de la Haute Couture Parisienne. Couture houses are under the leadership of a well-known couturier and specialize in designing, producing, and selling custom-made clothing. They are required to employ at least fifteen people and present two collections a year with no fewer than 35 ensembles for day and evening. The price of dresses and gowns ranges from $30,000 to $100,000, but the income from these sales is not enough to cover the cost of running a couture business. Currently, only about 2,000 women in the world are patrons of the traditional couture business, with approximately 200 as regular clients. Though the appeal of couture lies in its exclusivity, couturiers quickly understood that a broader base of customers was necessary for success. Many more women could experience the world of couture with the purchase of a bottle of perfume, and since World War I, the sale of perfumes and accessories has supported couture houses.

The Fédération Française de la Couture, du Prêt-à-porter des Couturiers et des Créateurs de Mode (French federation of fashion and of ready-to-wear of couturiers and fashion designers) governs the French fashion industry. It was created in 1973, from the existing Chambre Syndicale de la Haute Couture Parisienne, established in 1868. The federation has three separate divisions: (1) the Chambre Syndicale de la Haute Couture (syndicate chamber of high fashion); (2) the Chambre Syndicale de la Mode Masculine (syndicate chamber of men's ready-to-wear fashion), established in 1973; and (3) the Chambre Syndicale du Prêt-à-porter des Couturiers et des Créateurs de Mode (syndicate chamber of women's ready-to-wear of couturiers and fashion designers), established in 1973. The federation also has a fashion school, the Ecole de la Chambre Syndicale de la Couture Parisienne (school of the syndicate chamber of Parisian couture), which was created in 1928.

Couture collections are watched around the world, and though the couturiers do not dictate fashion trends, their houses perpetuate the tradition of luxury. With the freedom and support to experiment and push the boundaries of current fashion, they act as one set of visionaries in the fashion world. Historically, couturiers presented new fashions twice a year, and they had the power to dictate what was fashionable. Buyers from around the world came to view the collections and place orders for garments or toiles. Toiles had two purposes. The first was to be a test garment that would be used for fitting and perfecting the design for an individual client. It was part of the process of developing a finished garment. The second was to serve as the basis for another manufacturer to duplicate the couturier's originals, since the toiles were muslin copies of the dresses and suits that could be purchased.

Figure 1.1 Toile by Cristóbal Balenciaga, cotton muslin, 1950–1955, courtesy of the Goldstein Museum of Design, gift of Kathleen Catlin.

Manufacturers could interpret the toiles according to their own customers' taste and budget. The sale of original design concepts was an important part of the couture business; however, illegal copying has created problems for the couturier or designer, both past and present. (See chapter 4 for further discussion.)

One of the main reasons that women purchase couture clothing is for the experience. Visiting a couturier's atelier to order a custom-fitted and -designed garment was and still is considered the ultimate in luxury shopping. The ateliers are beautifully decorated, and each customer is served individually by a well-trained vendeuse who oversees the design selection, fittings, and delivery. She is the ultimate professional in customer service. Personal fashion shows and consultation with the designer are part of the experience. Regular customers have their own mannequins

Figure 1.2 Example of couture-quality construction in a dress by Laetitia, silk taffeta, 1955–1965, courtesy of the Goldstein Museum of Design, gift of Mary Ann Wark.

kept at the atelier. The garment that is delivered is constructed by hand with the finest fabrics and trims, and fits to perfection. It is considered an investment and will likely be worn for many years, even if refitting is required.

Today, designers from many countries work in the tradition of couture but are not formally part of the official of the Chambre Syndicale de la Couture Parisienne (syndicate chamber of Parisian couture). The 2010 members of the Chambre Syndicale include Adeline André, Anne Valérie Hash, Chanel, Christian Dior, Dominique Sirop, Franck Sorbier, Givenchy, Jean Paul Gaultier, Maurizio Galante, and Stephane Rolland, with correspondent members Elie Saab, Giorgio Armani, Maison Martin Margiela, and Valentino. Guest members are often included in the couture shows by invitation.

The originators

The following couturiers are a small selection of individuals who have had a lasting impact on the history of fashion design. They developed the framework from which the current fashion industry has grown. Their creativity, courage, and leadership introduced new methods of design, business, and promotion.

Charles Worth (1825–1895)

Charles Fredrick Worth is often called the grandfather of haute couture because his approach to dressing an elite clientele became a model for future couturiers. At the start of his career, Worth took advantage of the global inspiration that surrounded him in mid-nineteenth-century London, a center of international trade. Worth had flair for historic drama and, during several apprenticeships, developed talent for choosing fabrics and styles that flattered a woman. After a move to Paris, he took a position as chief cutter at Gagelin-Opigez. There, his reputation grew internationally as he won several gold medals at international design exhibitions. Worth started his own business in the rue de la Paix in 1858 and, with the patronage of the Princess Metternich, wife of the Austrian ambassador to Paris, became well connected to Empress Eugénie. Her political desire to promote textiles from Lyon led to Worth's commission to design all of her state and evening wear, enabling Worth to capitalize on his royal connections and develop his reputation for creativity and exclusivity. When Worth came to Paris and established his dressmaking business, he gave rise to the concept of "fashion designer" by putting his name on labels stitched into his garments. Worth established the Chambre Syndicale de la Haute Couture, which set the standards for future couturiers.

To manage sound retail practices and maintain dependable supply chains, Worth relied on his business partner, Otto Bobergh. They understood that an invisible but solid business understructure was essential. Though a Worth design could be identified by his use of texture, pattern, cut, and fine tailoring, it was the Worth name and image that attracted his women clients. The value of Worth as a couturier was the aura that surrounded him. His two sons, Jean-Philippe and Gaston, continued to build the business under the same philosophy of catering to select clients with aristocratic lifestyles. However, in 1901, Gaston moved to broaden the business in response to changing lifestyles that included less wealth and favored styles that allowed ease of movement. To accomplish this, he hired Paul Poiret.

Paul Poiret (1879–1944)

As a young boy, Paul Poiret fed his imagination while delivering umbrellas to Parisian department stores. Their lavish displays inspired his sketches, which he sold to local couturiers. Doucet (an established French couturier) hired him as an assistant, and he excelled at draping dramatic, seductive designs. His style attracted actresses Rejane and Sarah Bernhart, but unfortunately he was fired for designing garments for his actress mistress without the Doucet label. Artistic authorship was becoming a critical issue. The couturier is the person whose name is on the label and the door, regardless of who executes the actual design work. Poiret was then hired at Worth, but his designs were too revolutionary for Worth's traditional clients.

Poiret opened his own couture house in 1903. His marriage to Denise Boulet, whose family was in textile manufacturing, energized his work. As his muse, her youthful and adventurous attitudes led to his creation of the tubular Directoire line. This style retreated from the established standards of beauty, an hourglass shape created by wearing a corset, and embraced the idea of freedom of movement. Poiret was a leader in using radical sources of inspiration, including visual elements from the Far and Middle East, avant-garde contemporary painting, and the theater. Poiret's clothing had a fantasy spirit, and he reinforced this with grand, provocative parties such as "Thousand and Second Night" that created the image of an extravagant, luxurious lifestyle.

Poiret developed innovative promotional methods including a dress catalog with Iribe, a graphic artist who used stylized images that were flattened and highly decorated. In addition, his models made public appearances, and he hosted tours and showed films of fashion parades. In 1912, Poiret toured Europe and the United States to promote his work and found numerous unlicensed copies of his designs. This was due in part to his successful use of new promotional methods. When he returned home, Poiret worked to raise awareness of and combat design piracy with the French government. Unfortunately, his poor business practices and the decline of elite society following World War I caused him to collapse into bankruptcy.

Poiret depended on surface and texture to create interest in his simple shapes and forms. However, he is most respected for his role as a creative agent and his understanding of fashion promotion. With his successful media collaboration and his ability to suggest splendor and translate the idea of sexual desire, he "anticipated Hollywood and offered a showman's definition of fashion as dream" (Breward, 2003, 41).

Figure 1.3 Paul Iribe illustration of two Paul Poiret dresses, 1908.

Charles James (1906–1978)

Charles James was a fashion engineer. He sculpted fabric by building a structure that supported garments so that they appeared light and moved with grace. Though not part of the Paris couture, he could perhaps be called the first American couturier—with an international perspective. Born in England, he moved to Chicago and opened a millinery shop, experimenting with sculptural hat forms. He gained knowledge and experience with moves to New York, Paris, London, and back to New York in 1940. He had a reputation as a perfectionist, but he was also passionate and impetuous. Approaching shapes and structures with mathematical precision, his focused effort to raise fashion to a form of pure art gave him a reputation

Figure 1.4 Black evening coat with gold lining by Charles James, silk satin, 1947–1953, courtesy of the Goldstein Museum of Design, gift of Margot Siegel.

as the "Einstein of fashion." James was a technical genius and developed unique solutions for setting sleeves and subtle interpretations of geometric forms that have been compared to Cristóbal Balenciaga. He worked to extremes with designs that required many pieces or only a few to achieve their structure. He made use of solid fabrics to accentuate the cut, and lined garments with unexpected, vivid colors. He was fascinated by mass production but had difficulty making alterations to his designs to enable industry methods. He did work successfully with William Popper, a coat and suit manufacturer. Popper was able to capture the spirit of James's cut and color in ready-to-wear (RTW) that the designer could support. Though James produced only about 1,000 designs in his entire career, he is considered responsible for raising apparel design from an applied to a pure art form.

Madeleine Vionnet (1876–1975)

Madeleine Vionnet began her professional career with training as a dressmaker in Paris. Her primary interest was in learning the craft of clothing construction. After managing a dressmaker's shop in London, she returned to Paris and worked for the houses of Callot Sœurs and Jacques Doucet before opening her own salon in 1912. Her style developed in contrast to her background in English tailoring. Fluidity and complexity became her trademarks as she developed her designs directly on wooden half-scale forms. Her ability to view the body as a three-dimensional form and manipulate fabrics around that form resulted in truly innovative concepts. Her interest in working with geometric forms was expressed in the shapes she adapted to the body as well as the use of geometrically printed fabrics that reflected the futurist or cubist aesthetics of the time. Vionnet is best known for her use of the bias cut, which allowed for great freedom of movement and expression, though she did not originate the cut. The popularity of classicism in the 1930s allowed Vionnet to highlight her draping skills as her designs took inspiration from the Greek peplos.

Vionnet often felt challenged by the fashion marketplace and dealing with commercial issues, but she was innovative and proactive in her response. Illegal copies of her work were a threat even though her designs were difficult to copy. The designs, with unusual twists and interior constructions, made sense only when on a body, and it required expertise to wear them correctly. As a result, she produced a biannual photographic record of her collections that included front, back, and side views, with a code number and a fingerprint on every authorized product. She also had great compassion and concern for her workers. The latest technologies were used in her workrooms, and she provided health and social support. Vionnet retired in 1939, just prior to World War II. She was a gifted, hands-on designer, adept at the sophisticated interaction of fabric with the body.

Elsa Schiaparelli (1890–1973)

Elsa Schiaparelli had an unconventional view of the world and believed that women should dress to attract attention. When a buyer happened to see Schiaparelli wearing a black jersey dress with a trompe l'oeil bow, she placed a large order and Schiaparelli's design business was launched. By 1928, she had good press and a loyal clientele who wore her knits that clung to the body and trompe l'oeil accessories. A year later, she opened her first boutique. Inspired by surrealist art, she embraced the idea of paradox as she experimented with the structure, material, and function of familiar garments, such as waistcoats made from horse blankets, jodhpurs for skiing, and tweed for evening wear. Her social circle included avant-garde artists, Marcel Duchamp, Picabia, Alfred Stieglitz, Paul Poiret, and Man Ray. Schiaparelli collaborated with Salvador Dali and Jean Cocteau to develop thematic collections in which they integrated details such as lips, hair, hands, shoes, toys, and candy on the garment to shock the viewer. Her shoe hat and lobster dress collaborations with Dali found a striking balance between surreal commentary and amusing fashion.

With her heightened sense of theater, Schiaparelli established strong relationships in Hollywood. As an example, her 1938 perfume Shocking was presented in a bottle shaped like Mae West, a curvaceous actress. After World War II and a period in New York, she returned to Paris but was not welcomed by the Chambre Syndicale de la Haute Couture. Her style of irony and provocation did not complement the new conservative trends popular after the war, and her salon closed in 1945.

With shocking pink as her signature color, Schiaparelli delighted in outrageous style. Her eclectic vision was supported by a deep understanding of the world and the unconscious fashion psyche, which she used to express her avant-garde creativity. By mixing art and fashion she presented a model for collaborative work and offered women the opportunity to dress with humor, delight, and confidence.

Figure 1.5 Cream and navy "tree bark" evening dress by Elsa Schiaparelli, silk matalesse, 1938, courtesy of the Goldstein Museum of Design.

Christian Dior (1905–1957)

Christian Dior's contribution to couture was brief, but the impact of his vision has been extensive. His debut collection, the Corolle line, was presented on February 12, 1947. The silhouette of a slim waist, high bust, round shoulders, and full hips was called the "new look" by Carmel Snow, the editor-in-chief of *Harper's Bazaar*. This dramatic, feminine change that dropped hemlines nine inches and used lavish fabrics, trims, and a well-built understructure created a sensation for Dior. Though initially rejected by women who protested about the amount of fabric used after the limitations of World War II, he knew that they were ready to be more feminine and rediscover the pleasures of being a woman. With this change in vision, Dior was able to return Paris to its position as fashion leader after the devastation of the war.

Dior studied politics, but his lifelong passion was for the arts. He opened an art gallery for a short time, until his family lost their fortune. Dior was able to sell fashion

Figure 1.6 Coral and white tweed suit by Christian Dior, wool, 1960–1965, courtesy of the Goldstein Museum of Design, gift of Sarah E. Lindsay.

sketches to haute couture houses until he found a job as an assistant to the couturier Robert Piguet. Later he worked as primary designer for Lucien Lelong, with Pierre Balmain as a coworker. He opened his own house in 1946 with financial backing from Marcel Boussac, a cotton-fabric mogul. Dior developed a new business model by establishing Dior as a global brand that included his wholesale business Christian Dior-New York Inc. in 1948, organizing a perfume company, and designing cashmere sweaters for Scotland's Hawick looms and bathing suits for Cole of California. When a U.S. hosiery company offered $10,000 for the rights to manufacture Dior stockings, Dior proposed receiving a percentage of the product's sales, thus introducing the royalty system to fashion. Dior died in 1957 at the height of his career, with a name known all over the world and his label making up half of France's haute couture exports. Dior was a gentleman of good taste with an appreciation of art, culture, and beauty, but his legacy, beyond the New Look, will be his business acumen.

Gabrielle "Coco" Chanel (1883–1971)

Gabrielle "Coco" Chanel made her fortune from Chanel No. 5 perfume. This first perfume bearing a designer's name was launched in 1923 and sold in a bottle that exemplified her design work: simple and elegant. Raised as an orphan and trained as a milliner, she began to develop her style of hidden luxury that used wardrobe opposites to draw attention to her designs. The knits that had traditionally been worn only by the working class became a casual yet elegant base for her opulent costume jewelry. She was groundbreaking in her embrace of comfort as she took masculine ideas of dress and made them feminine with knit pieces in neutral colors. Chanel took inspiration from the recreational lifestyle of the rich and participated in that lifestyle with the support of a series of wealthy suitors that created a public persona full of rumors and turmoil. She was well aware of the image she had created and used it to her advantage to market the lifestyle of an elite fashion designer. Like many other designers of the time, she was involved with many film and theater projects that included Gloria Swanson, Jean Renoir, Jean Cocteau, and the Ballets Russe.

The name Chanel became associated with the modernization of women's clothing. Her little black dress was the Model T of fashion, and while she did license her name to retail companies, it was her perfumes, jewelry, and accessories that built the Chanel global fashion business. After World War II, she had some difficulty reestablishing herself following rumors of an association with the Nazis and the strong trend toward the New Look, whose formality and curvilinear form was so opposite her style of casual, elegant luxury. She did reopen her fashion house in 1954 and was extremely successful in the American market with her boucle suits and trademark quilted handbag until she died in 1971. In 1957 at the Fashion Awards in Dallas, Texas, the fashion world honored her as the most influential designer of the twentieth century. Chanel independently addressed the needs of the modern urban woman by presenting simplicity and elegance in dress that, above all, was comfortable. She authorized fashionable, elegant, and functional styles for women that are still worn today.

Figure 1.7. Red, white, and black suit by Gabrielle "Coco" Chanel, wool houndstooth, wool jersey, 1955, courtesy of the Goldstein Museum of Design, gift of Ed and Lois Schlampp.

Cristóbal Balenciaga (1895–1972)

Cristóbal Balenciaga was a shape genius and master of color. He introduced a dramatic shift in the fashionable silhouette of the late 1950s that used proportion as the guiding design element. Both the sack dress and the chemise lacked a defined waist but were embraced as complimentary to many body types. Ready-to-wear manufacturers developed similar designs at every price point. Balenciaga's training as a tailor, along with his understanding of sculpture and the very high standards that he set for himself, resulted in a beautiful purity of line. Spain was an inspiration for Balenciaga throughout his career, particularly the art and vestments of the Catholic Church. He opened his first house in 1919 in the fashionable resort of San Sebastian, where he had learned tailoring, and expanded to three additional shops. During the Spanish Civil War in 1937, he moved to Paris and opened an atelier with the confidence to express his own innovative ideas independent of the trends. As a Spanish speaker in Paris, he was very private and gave few interviews to the press.

Though his designs are deceptively simple in line, some knowledge of tailoring is needed to fully appreciate his clothes. His modern and dramatic designs were patronized by the Duchess of Westminster and supported by major American department stores. He was well known for his unique color combinations of black and brown or black lace over bright pink. Balenciaga's use of heavy fabrics, tailoring skills, and bold materials allowed him to achieve a fluidity in his designs that is his alone. With the help of the Swiss fabric house of Abraham, he developed silk gazar, a stiff but pliable fabric. Balenciaga's experimentation with volume, shading,

Figure 1.8 Black silk gazar evening dress with cape by Cristóbal Balenciaga, 1960–1965, courtesy of the Goldstein Museum of Design.

texture, and historical reference gave his work a distinctive elegance that often revealed unusual erogenous zones such as the wrist or the base of the neck. His influence is evident in the work of Courreges and Ungaro, who apprenticed with him. His sense of success was measured against his own high standards, but his expensive techniques and the disappearing lifestyle of couture led to his retirement in 1968.

The changing role of couture

From the mid-nineteenth century until the 1960s, haute couture was the main fashion industry. Though much of the early twentieth century was dedicated to political and economic growth and controversy, haute couture survived despite frequent interruptions and challenges. Lifestyles began to change dramatically in the 1960s as women began to work in greater numbers, became better informed, and had more control over their income. As a result, haute couture went out of fashion. Travel became easier and more popular; thus the same wardrobe could be worn in multiple locations because it hadn't been seen before, and with busier lives, women were not willing to wait weeks and endure hours of fitting for a couture dress. There was also a new focus on youth culture whose styles were radically different from the more mature styles of the couture houses.

A transition was taking place that moved power from the Paris couturiers to the individual woman who was free to choose her own style. With no fashion absolutes, a new perspective was required for those who wished to continue the tradition of haute couture. The couture business continues to serve a small part of the population who are interested in custom-designed couture garments. Since the early 1970s, most couture houses have operated at a financial loss. Couture houses today are more focused on growing their brand and the underlying business. The lavish display of luxury on the runway is often justified because it creates sensational visibility for the brand that supports the sale of other products with the house label. Haute couture is also used as a way to experiment with new ideas that may eventually be used for prêt-à-porter (RTW) collections.

Today, a couturier must have a vision, a personality, and a strong business backing. Couturiers' responsibility is to help create an image that supports the brand name, and many are viewed as celebrities. Most couture houses are no longer under the direction of the name of the house; however, the names of the old couturiers hold great value. Only a few current couturiers design under their own label. While some have been involved with philanthropic ventures, there is little voice for social responsibility. Business concerns appear to take precedence for both the Moderns and the Next Generation couturier designers. The following are modern couturiers who have carried the tradition of haute couture into the twenty-first century, with most extending their work to prêt-à-porter lines and the business of the brand.

Hubert de Givenchy (1927–)

Hubert de Givenchy's reputation for elegance began with his first collection, which was made entirely of white men's shirting fabric. The collection was a success, despite his lack of funding, in response to the casual chic design and introduction of separates. With Balenciaga as his mentor and experience working with Fath, Piguet, Lelong, and Schiaparelli, he designed elegant, fresh, ladylike garments. Balenciaga helped him to mature as a couturier, teaching him how to minimize, avoid unnecessary detail, and use shape and color.

Givenchy is well known for dressing two American style icons: Audrey Hepburn and Jackie Kennedy. He met Hepburn when the costumes for the movie *Sabrina* needed to be redesigned, and though he expected Katharine Hepburn, Givenchy and Audrey began a long relationship in which they developed the look of the ingénue. She also became the face of his perfume L'Interdit. Mrs. Kennedy wore a Givenchy dress in 1961 during an official visit to France, and he dressed her for many other occasions, including the funeral of John F. Kennedy.

In 1954, Givenchy, an excellent businessman, was the first to present a high-end prêt-à-porter line designed by a couturier. In an effort to prevent counterfeiting, he and Balenciaga presented their collections to both clients and the press simultaneously, and this has become a continued practice in the industry since 1956. Though encouraged by his friend and mentor Balenciaga to avoid licensing agreements, Givenchy set up licenses to expand into home textiles, accessories, and cars, including a Ford Lincoln Continental, to support his couture business. In 1968, Givenchy opened Givenchy Nouvelle Boutique, where he sold his more light-hearted but still elegant prêt-à-porter line. For the next twenty years, Givenchy continued to design elegant clothing for a large clientele. Givenchy sold his house to Moët Hennessy - Louis Vuitton (LVMH) in 1988 and retired in 1995. The house has had several designers since, including John Galliano, Alexander McQueen, Julien MacDonald, and currently Riccardo Tisci, who seems to have the refined, gentle Givenchy attitude.

Valentino Garavani (1932–)

Valentino Garavani is best known for his opulent dresses and his signature color, *rosso Valentino*. He is a master of elegance and beauty, combining the couture of Paris and Italy, using French embroidery and Italian fabrics. Valentino studied fashion in Milan and Paris and then worked for Dessès and Laroche. He opened his own house in Rome in 1959 but achieved worldwide recognition with his 1962 show in Florence. His no-color collection was a risk at a time when electric color was in vogue, but it presented both a power and subtlety that earned him the Neiman Marcus award. Discovered by celebrities who visited Rome to shoot films in the early 1960s, including *Dolce Vita*, directed by Federico Fellini, he was called the

Golden Boy of Italian couture and often referred to this time as his "sweet life." Valentino dressed new and established celebrities and royalty throughout his career. Wedding dresses were a specialty of his, and he designed one for Jacqueline Kennedy when she married Aristotle Onassis in 1968, and for Jennifer Lopez for her marriage to Marc Anthony in 2001.

Valentino's first prêt-à-porter boutique opened in Milan in 1969, followed by another in Rome. In the 1970s his initial "V" became a logo on his products, and he began a partnership with Giancarlo Giammetti, whose business expertise led to the house's expansion and success. As a result, they were able to found the Academie Valentino in 1989, a cultural center for art exhibitions and cultural activities. And, with the profits from the center, they established IIFE (Italian for "Fighting, Informing, Building, Teaching"), an association to support AIDS patients. In 1998, Valentino sold his company to Holding di Partecipazioni Industriali (HdP) and remained

Figure 1.9 Cream dress by Valentino, wool, 1990–1999, courtesy of the Goldstein Museum of Design, gift of Brenda Stowers.

as the designer. He believed that this would give the Valentino name longevity. Four years later, HdP sold Valentino to Marzotto, another Italian luxury goods group. Valentino announced his retirement and completed his last haute couture collection in January 2008, naming as his successor Alessandra Facchinetti. As a designer with impeccable taste and workmanship, Valentino stands out for his excellence in serving his clientele. He has been called the last survivor of the great days of haute couture, though he embraced the new role of couture with success.

Giorgio Armani (1934–)

Giorgio Armani knows how to make a suit. His reputation is built on his ability to transform the wearer by tailoring the most comfortable, fluid jacket, resulting in a feeling of confidence, comfort, and sensuality. Using a neutral palette, Armani's style is elegant and at the same time down-to-earth. He began his career in fashion as a window dresser and buyer, and he gained experience working for Nino Cerruti for nine years. He established Giorgio Armani S.p.A. with his partner Sergio Galeotti in 1974, starting with menswear and adding women's wear the next year. Armani's business grew rapidly as he added multiple RTW lines targeted at different customers. His reputation grew when he designed for Richard Gere in the movie *American Gigolo*. Armani was one of the first designers to approach celebrities to wear his designs, beginning with the former Los Angeles Lakers basketball coach Pat Riley. His business sense was excellent as he diversified into perfume, eyewear, hotels, restaurants, and sports teams. *Time* magazine honored him with a cover in 1982 in recognition of his design and business expertise. In 2005, for the first time in Paris, Armani showed his new line Haute Couture Prive, a well-received collection of glamorous and graceful evening gowns. In January 2007, he became the first designer to broadcast a haute couture fashion show live on the Internet via Microsoft Corporation's MSN and Cingular cellular phones.

Armani also has a humanitarian sense of style. His concern for others is seen in his support for banning models with a body mass index (BMI) under 18. The normal range is 20–25. He was recognized as a Goodwill Ambassador by the United Nations in 2002 for his work with Afghan refugees and was named the "Best Dressed Environmentalist" by the Sustainable Style Foundation. In 2005, Armani sold 75 percent of A/X Armani Exchange, one of his ready-to-wear lines, to Como Holdings in an effort to expand into a more moderate market. He has been honored with an exposition at the Guggenheim Museum that traveled to five other world venues. His innovative tailoring sets a new standard for prestige and glamour.

Yves Saint Laurent (1936–2008)

Yves Saint Laurent was a creative genius who viewed fashion as both elegant and democratic. He helped to define a new view of fashion for a consumer who was no longer interested in traditional haute couture. Saint Laurent trained at the Ecole de la Chambre Syndicale de la Couture Parisienne and then worked with Dior until the latter's death in 1957. At the age of twenty-one, Saint Laurent became a very young chief designer for the house of Dior. In contrast to Dior, his first collection, the Trapeze line, had a softer, more relaxed view that reflected his vision while still respecting the house's tradition. After a difficult period in the army, he opened his own house in 1962, financed by his companion, Pierre Bergé, where he could develop more radical collections based on his creative perspective as a left-bank bohemian. He developed a style of presenting themed collections that ranged from Africa to Russia to pop culture and worked to develop a timeless look using the natural line of the female body. One of his most enduring contributions was the empowerment of women with the tailored trouser suit. The safari jacket, art dresses inspired by Picasso and Mondrian, the sheer blouse, and the jumpsuit also stand out as innovative concepts that were reflective of the time and timeless. Saint Laurent also had an extraordinary sense of color and was willing to break the rules as he combined orange/pink/red, black/ brown, and light blue/olive green/orange.

In an attempt to democratize fashion and popularize prêt-à-porter, he launched the Rive Gauche line and boutique with less expensive clothing. Saint Laurent and his YSL logo have translated well to the perfume and accessories that contribute to a profitable international company. In 1968, his collection was dedicated to student radicals protesting capitalist activities, but in the following years his work became quieter and more responsive to society's norms. His name is associated with a jet-set lifestyle and fragile sensitivity; for example, in a promotion for his men's fragrance, he posed nude as a celebration of sexuality without a note of scandal. Saint Laurent's fresh view in the early 1960s was directed away from the New Look and presented clothing that was inspired by women living in a rapidly changing society with a focus on democracy, equality, and a global view.

Jean Paul Gaultier (1952–)

Jean Paul Gaultier is a showman. He embraces controversy and holds unconventional ideas about beauty and ugliness. Using humor and irony to challenge our view of the world, Gaultier is considered one of our most important designers. Based on sketches he sent to all the major designers, a young Gaultier was invited to work with Pierre Cardin for a year. He returned to work for Cardin in the Philippines four years later, after working at Patou and Esterel. Gaultier presented his first couture collection with his partner Kashiyama in 1978. Over the next ten years, he presented concepts using unexpected materials such as imitation leather, wood, garbage, and nonwoven fabrics. He brought high fashion to the masses and street style to the runway. Known as the enfant terrible of French fashion, he gained respect when he received the Paris Fashion Oscar in 1987. The following year saw the first evidence of his obsession with the corset, and the world was jolted when he designed a corset with conical breasts for Madonna for her 1990 Blond Ambition tour. This corset concept was carried through in the bottle for his first perfume, Jean Paul Gaultier Parfum, based on Schiaparelli's bottle of Shocking.

Gaultier uses a variety of ethnic and fantasy inspirations with playful, gender-bending interpretations for both men and women. His original presentations are theatrical, and many designers have followed his lead in creating an experience, not just a fashion show. He is a skillful designer who works at the cutting edge using classic silhouettes to ground his experiments. Gaultier believes that styles and construction have not kept pace with technology, and thus changes are imminent. Hermes has financed 35 percent of Gaultier's business since 1999, and in May 2003, Gaultier became the chief designer at Hermes. Up to that point, he had designed only for his own label. That same year, Gaultier staged a retrospective exhibition at the Victoria and Albert Museum, following the lead of Saint Laurent at the Metropolitan Museum of Art (1983), Issey Miyake (1998) at the Fondation Cartier pour l'Art Contemporain, and Armani at the Guggenheim (in 2000). The fashion world has great respect for Gaultier and his ability to mix the serious skills of a couturier with the creative genius of a rebel spirit.

SPOTLIGHT ON MUSEUM COLLECTIONS: THE VICTORIA AND ALBERT MUSEUM

The Victoria and Albert Museum wants to inspire those who shape contemporary design. As a resource for fashionable dress from the seventeenth century to the present day, with an emphasis on progressive and influential designs from the major fashion centers of Europe, the Victoria and Albert is a treasure for current designers and students. Garments are engaging because the viewer is captured by both the visual excitement and the hidden story of the garments, creating a dynamic connection to the designer, the wearer, and the time. The artifact has historical value, but the physical details, such as the texture and drape of the fabric or the detail of the stitching, present less obvious information about the intricacies of design.

The Victoria and Albert will work with designers to arrange a visit to view specific garments, but a wealth of inspiration is available on a daily basis by exploring the costume displays as well as the other areas of the museum. There is often an exhibit of student work on display or a live show in progress. Their online sources are an excellent way to start research or preview the collection. A 360-degree view is available for some garments. The National Art Library located in the Victoria and Albert is also available for research. The luxury of visiting the Victoria and Albert to sketch, reflect, and allow connections to form is an important investment for designers. There is no better way to explore and understand the history of fashion or find inspiration for future projects.

Christian Lacroix (1951–)

Christian Lacroix is a master of exuberant color, lavish in his use of fabric, embroidery, and flowers. So strong is his love of bright colors that his Spring 2003 collection made headlines for his first use of black. Born in 1951 in the south of France, he studied art history at the Sorbonne University, Paris. He began his career as a fashion sketcher and assistant at Hermes. He made a great impact in 1981 when he joined Jean Patou and revamped the company, tripling sales. In 1986 Lacroix was awarded the *De d'or* (golden thimble) for his couture collection, and a year later, he received the Oscar for the Best Foreign Designer from the Council of Fashion Designers of America. Lacroix opened his own haute couture salon in 1987, the first to open in Paris in two decades. His introduction of the "pouf" and his use of sumptuous fabrics and overlapping patterns became icons of the 1980s. Financed by LVMH, he led one of their fastest-growing brands with the addition of a prêt-à-porter collection, perfume, and the development of his "Luxe" line. Accessories and home furnishings were added, along with the BAZAR line of youthful, funky casual wear. He designed uniforms for the crew of Air France that enhance the elegant image of the airline, and his sense of color is evident in the interior of the French National Railway's high-speed trains.

Though influenced by historical fashion, Lacroix is modern in his approach to design and presentation. He often designs fabrics digitally and sent out a CD to buyers and press with the looks from his Spring 2004 RTW collection. Instead of a show, in 2002, he sent invitations to an intimate dinner showing pieces from his signature jeans and BAZAR lines with some vintage couture gowns, quietly demonstrating his range as a designer. He became artistic director of Pucci from 2002 to 2005 and then began a fresh start when LVMH sold the house. Lacroix has a light spirit and seems to preserve the true nature of haute couture, with imagination, confidence, and Parisian sophistication.

The couture house of Christian Lacroix filed for bankruptcy, and as of March 2010, the Lacroix name was licensed. Jean-jacques Picart, fashion business consultant, attributes the failure to poor management. He has hope that Lacroix, even without his name, may find success using a niche strategy with a smaller, more exclusive focus that is more sustainable (McNicoll, 2010).

FASHION FOCUS FROM THE FIELD: RALPH RUCCI

As the first American designer to be invited to show at the Paris haute couture shows since Mainbocher in the 1930s, Ralph Rucci exemplifies the technique, tenacity, and vision required of a great designer. The 2002 invitation from the Chambre Syndicale de la Haute Couture came after twenty years in business. Motivated by the anatomy and movement of the female body, Rucci developed a focus on cutting clothes to follow the lines of the body, providing a feeling of sensuality and fluidity.

Rucci believes that research is the most important part of his work. His notebooks are a rich collection of notes, images, and sketches that he uses to translate ideas into wearable clothes. He studied at the Fashion Institute of Technology and took advantage of the costume collections at the Metropolitan Museum of Art to analyze the work of Cristóbal Balenciaga, Madame Grés, and Charles James. He started his career at Halston, eventually opening his own business in 1981, but he was forced to close when an order was canceled mid-production after a drop in the stock market. By 1994, he started a new company called Chado, borrowing the name from the Japanese tea ceremony associated with grace and serenity. Throughout his career, he has been committed to making clothes that respect the idea of individuality and highlight the movement of the female body. This is achieved with great attention, respect, and continued innovation within the craft of dressmaking.

The next generation

Still respected as a valuable tradition, haute couture has been slow to adapt to societal changes. The constant struggle to finance the luxury of a couture business has led many new designers to establish themselves in the stronger prêt-à-porter or RTW markets. Business survival and growth, in addition to their craft, remain the focus of practicing couturiers. Most have not adopted a voice of social responsibility, which is more commonly heard from RTW designers. Couturiers' contribution may be the preservation of a disappearing craft or the introduction of a new direction. The following couturiers appear to be the future of haute couture. While they are extremely talented, their vision and leadership are yet undeveloped; thus the future of haute couture remains unknown.

Dominique Sirop (1956–)

Dominique Sirop defines his style as "minimalist dandy" and works to combine sophistication and simplicity in his designs. He is inspired by his mother, who was a couturier's mannequin for the House of Paquin, and began his career as an apprentice at Yves Saint Laurent at the age of seventeen. Givenchy brought Sirop onto his team in 1978, and twelve years later, he started designing for Hanae Mori. Sirop is well known for his cocktail dresses, and his work focuses on blending the traditional craft of couture with the development of new fabrics and technologies. His work is futuristic in tone and enhances the sensuality of a woman's body. Sirop has a passion for fashion history and has authored the books *A Historical Overview of the House of Paquin* (1989) and *Jacqueline Delubac* (1994). As an expert on the history of costume, he is often consulted by museums, providing a valuable service to the preservation of our material culture.

In September 1996, Sirop opened his own couture house, and less than one year later, the Chambre Syndicale de la Haute Couture invited him to be a member. He grew the business in a partnership with Daimaru shops in Japan to produce the prêt-à-porter line Dominique Sirop for Daimaru, and a partnership with the jeweler Cartier. He continues to work in his atelier on the 14th rue du Faubourg Saint Honore. Creativity and perfection are at the core of his designs, and his role in haute couture will be worth watching.

Elie Saab (1964–)

Opulent fabrics, lace, and embroidery, enhanced with pearls and crystals, are the elements that Elie Saab uses to create his collections of evening and bridal gowns. His designs are synonymous with luxury and elegance, and his ability to fuse European trends and Middle Eastern inspiration results in distinct, modern designs with an international appeal. He was born and works in Beirut, Lebanon, where he set up his atelier in 1982, bypassing his original intention to study fashion in Paris. His reputation and business grew, and in 1997 Saab was the first non-Italian designer to become a member of the Italian Camera Nazionale della Moda (national chamber for Italian fashion).

Saab's visibility increased in 2002 when Halle Berry wore his burgundy gown to receive the Oscar for Best Actress. The following year, the Fédération Française de la Couture announced that Saab had been invited to present his first Paris haute couture collection. Saab continued to expand his business with the presentation of a prêt-à-porter collection in 2005. He was nominated as a correspondent member by the Chambre Syndicale de la Haute Couture in 2006, placing him firmly in the exclusive haute couture. Saab has a powerful vision that is both feminine and alluring. Experimenting with the themes of femininity and romanticism places Saab in a unique position to make women feel beautiful. The use of materials and the cut of the gowns to fit the curves of a woman's body are this designer's strength.

Anne Valérie Hash (1971–)

Inspired to use deconstructed menswear as a starting point, Anne Valérie Hash has built a strong reputation by reenvisioning and reshaping masculine pieces for the female body. Following her graduation from the Ecole de la Chambre Syndicale de la Couture Parisienne in 1995, she studied art and design at Temple University in Philadelphia, Pennsylvania. Hash continued learning about the industry with work as an intern at Lacroix, Dior, Nina Ricci, Chanel, and Chloe. Two years after presenting her first collection in 2001, from which no sales were made, she received the prestigious ANDAM Award for a promising young fashion designer. She has developed a method of working that starts by undoing the seams in men's jackets and trousers and draping the pieces around a young girl model to facilitate her experimentation with proportions. She then reconstructs the garments in adult sizes.

Invited to join the Chambre Syndicale de la Haute Couture, she presented her first couture collection in July 2007. She and Adeline André are the only women among the fifteen members. Hash continues to move toward a more feminine aesthetic by adding materials that are light, delicate, and fluid to a strong sartorial base. Her children's collection, Mademoiselle, expands her business, though she has purposely kept her company small as insurance against her earlier experiences with financial hardship. As a woman who designs for women and children, her work is likely to evolve in a fresh direction as her talents and experience grow. Hash's arty, playful interpretation of feminine and masculine is a powerful and practical voice.

Prêt-à-porter

Prêt-à-porter is the French term for the highest level of RTW, and this sector is governed by the Chambre Syndicale du Prêt-à-porter des Couturiers et des Créateurs de Mode. Couturiers have used prêt-à-porter to expand and support their haute couture business, and créateurs (designers) design exclusively for prêt-à-porter, without a couture line. The prêt-à-porter lines are sold in flagship boutiques or department store boutiques. The boutiques reflect the image of the couturier's house or the designer, and the garments carry the house's label. Many outstanding designers create prêt-à-porter lines, including Sonia Rykiel, Stella McCartney, Junya Wantanabe, and Dries Van Noten. High-quality design and fabrics, along with quality industrial construction, make these garments desirable beyond the brand image. Customer service and fitting services are included in the purchase of prêt-à-porter garments.

Mass producers of prêt-à-porter or RTW began originally by copying couture garments. In 1963, a new category of designers began to emerge. Stylists developed designs based on what the average woman wanted to wear, and these RTW businesses were very successful in attracting foreign buyers. The stylists brought a young, bohemian sense to their garments. Though they were inexperienced in comparison to the couturiers, the stylists were hired by major fashion houses. By the mid-1960s it was no longer considered inappropriate to purchase a RTW garment off the rack. Many couturiers began to show both a couture line and a prêt-à-porter line. However, haute couture was losing ground, and tensions rose. The couturiers felt that the stylists did not know what they were doing, and the stylists felt that the couturiers were copying them. Ready-to-wear continued to improve, and most new young stylists, now referred to as designers, were attracted to that sector of the industry. In 1973, five Americans were invited to show in Paris, along with five French designers, to support the Versailles Restoration Fund. Bill Blass, Halston, Stephan Burrows, Anne Klein, and Oscar de la Renta showcased the strength of RTW American sportswear. The same year, the Japanese designers Kenzo Takada and Issey Miyake showed their lines for the first time in Paris. This introduced a much more global view of fashion, though the Paris runways are still considered the pinnacle of success.

Fashion, in its broadest sense, is the clothing that we choose to wear at any point in time. Something is fashionable if it exemplifies the current culture and lifestyle. For example, the miniskirt of the 1960s represented women's freedom and the importance of youth in society. The pantsuit of the 1970s advanced the call for women's equality. Fashion also depends on our resources and needs, both as a society and as individuals. Thus fashion exists on a continuum from clothing that serves the very basic need to cover the body for protection and modesty to the very avant-garde or intellectual fashion as art. Most of what we know about historical fashion represents the wealthy or royal individuals of the time. They had the resources, in both time and money, and the desire to differentiate themselves from other classes. For those less fortunate, there was a style of acceptable and affordable dress, but the concepts of fashion and differentiation were not a priority. In the last 200 years of Western fashion, dressing fashionably has become a democratic process.

In the nineteenth century, the ability to purchase fabrics and supplies for home or private dressmaking increased as society moved toward a more industrialized economy. Fashion magazines circulated and fashion dolls were sent to publicize the latest looks from Paris, the capital of fashion. Change occurred, but it was not rapid, as communication and travel were limited and time-consuming.

Paris couturiers dictated the details and silhouettes of fashion for over 100 years. A different source of fashion began to evolve as Mary Quant opened the Bazaar boutique in the mid-1950s and sold her handmade miniskirts, while many others in London and New York experimented with an infusion of global aesthetics. However, in the 1960s a true revolution in fashion began. The focus shifted from the Paris couturiers to a youth culture that was exciting, political, and modern. It was a time of revolt and contradictions, with an appreciation of handmade clothing and crafts, ethnic groups, folklore, and alternative religions. Fashion ideas came from the street and went up the fashion pyramid. Jeans became an enduring part of fashion: an equalizing uniform for both the masses and the elite.

Fashion has advanced from the beautiful but mostly unattainable garments of the haute couture to more available, pleasurable, and disposable displays of style. In the mid-twentieth century, new fibers that were less expensive and required less care were more widely used, including polyester, nylon, and acrylic. There was much more interest in producing clothing for the mass market, because it was smart business. Today, fashion is accessible immediately as it happens, with clips of fashion shows being posted on the Internet mere hours after the event. Fashion is also accessible at every price point. For example, the major retailer Target promotes the concept of "Design for All" as it offers an ever-changing array of clothing from current designers. Anyone can put together a fashionable outfit whether they purchase it at Selfridges or Sears. Most important, there is a great variety of choice for consumers, and they are free to decide on a style that suits them.

Summary

- Haute couture was born by providing luxury, custom-fitted garments to aristocratic society, and it is governed by the Chambre Syndicale de la Haute Couture Parisienne.
- The sale of perfumes and accessories supported the traditional couture house, as it does today, with the addition of prêt-à-porter.
- The couturiers Worth, Poiret, Chanel, and Dior developed the business and promotional expertise to advance the concept and profitability of couture.
- James, Vionnet, and Balenciaga are respected for their technical expertise and elevating the craft of couture.
- Schiaparelli was a collaborator with an adventurous voice.
- The Moderns—Givenchy, Valentino, Armani, Saint Laurent, and Gaultier—maintain the traditions of haute couture while transitioning into a shifting culture of fashion.
- The changing lifestyles of women and a new focus on youth culture contributed to a change in haute couture and supported the development of the RTW industry.
- Sirop, Saab, and Hash are part of haute couture's Next Generation who are preserving the traditions of haute couture.
- Today, haute couture supports the development of the brand by creating an image of luxury and individuality.
- The democracy of fashion has advanced with the help of industrialization, technology, and the youth culture, and it indicates the value of choice for the consumer.

Vocabulary

- atelier
- bohemian
- gazar
- haute couture
- prêt-à-porter
- ready-to-wear
- toile
- trompe l'oeil
- vendeuse

Discussion

1. Is there a future for haute couture in the twenty-first century? Justify your answer.
2. Discuss the relationship between art and fashion.
3. How has war impacted haute couture?
4. What are the qualities a couturier needs to be successful today?
5. What is the value of regulating membership in the Chambre Syndicale de la Haute Couture?
6. Why isn't Gaultier part of the Next Generation haute couture?
7. To be successful, is it more important to be creative or have a strong business sense?
8. What are the ethical concerns of couture fashion?
9. What have we lost and what have we gained from the changes in the traditional haute couture?

2

HOW APPAREL IS DEVELOPED

What does it take to transform a sketch of a garment into the real thing? It starts with an idea, but before a designer can begin sketching, a wealth of information is needed to guide the creative process. Designers must to be aware of the world around them and the world at a distance. What's going on in the world of fashion with trends, designers, and collections is important. Even more important is what is going on outside of fashion and in the life of your target consumer. How would you describe the economic outlook, lifestyle, and values of your customers? What are their physical, functional, and social needs related to apparel? Where do they live, work, and shop? What are their dreams and aspirations? Do they have a family? Do they travel? Is the garment being produced overseas or right in your own design studio? What are the cost and safety issues related to the garment you are designing? What is the news about the economic, political, and social issues in the world? How do the "megatrends" of our time influence design decisions? Designers will want to act like sponges and absorb everything they see, read, hear, touch, and feel. Good observation skills and the ability to make connections between outwardly unrelated ideas are important characteristics for all designers. Designers have responsibilities that extend beyond drawing new designs, and their foresight can translate into successful garments and companies. So whether a designer is designing for a large international company or for a small local clientele, this chapter will provide insight into the process of developing a garment.

Trend forecasting

Trends occur in the clothing we wear, the food we eat, and the way we communicate, travel, and spend our free time. There are even trends in what we value and how we view the world. Robyn Waters, "the Trendmaster," suggests looking at trends from the perspective of what's important, not just what's next (2005). Consumers' actions are often the most accurate indication of what they will do, much more so than what they say they will do. Observation is important to determine what people value with respect to how they spend their time, energy, and money. For example, if Anna is concerned about the environment, she may want to change the way she gets to work. This might mean taking the bus, riding her bike, or walking more. Translated into clothing, this might mean a trend toward wearing lower-heeled shoes, layers to accommodate increased exercise, or outerwear with better wind and rain resistance. Looking at this trend in a larger context might indicate a bigger demand for public transportation, more walker-friendly streets, or more bike racks at businesses and restaurants.

It is important to identify the megatrends, or all-encompassing shifts in society's values and actions that influence our lives and choices in a multitude of ways. Just knowing that next season lower-heeled shoes will be popular limits a designer's ability to respond to the trend in a way that addresses the needs of the target consumer. In contrast, knowing that there is a trend toward alternate forms of transportation based on a concern for the environment suggests many ways in which an apparel designer can respond to the consumer's needs.

Our world generally strives to be balanced, so in response to the big trends that occur, countertrends often develop. In response to fast food and eating on the run there is growing interest in the slow food movement where friends and families eat home-cooked meals together. Fast fashion that changes every few weeks is balanced by growing interest in clothing that has been around for a long time—both as vintage garments and recycled clothing. Being aware and noticing the paradoxes that occur in our world and even within an individual can reveal new opportunities for design.

Research

Identifying trends takes research and reflection. It also takes an enormous amount of time. This is one reason why designers are constantly observing their surroundings, even when they are not officially working. Designers usually require information about seasonal, lifestyle, and consumer trends; updates on fibers, fabrics, and production methods; inspiration; and new business opportunities. The information should be gathered and interpreted quickly to be useful to the designer. Continuous monitoring is a necessity in a world that is constantly changing. While an independent designer might be responsible for all the research needed, designers for larger companies have a variety of resources to collect information.

Where are the best sources of information? The explosion of resources on the Internet is currently the most timely and cost-effective means of acquiring current news. We now have access to runway-show pictures minutes after the live show occurs, breaking news from across the world, views of international cities and shops, commentary, and blogs. You can use resources and indexes from libraries, trade associations, or the government. E-mail, webinars, and live chats put you in touch with people who can answer questions, teach, or provide links to alternate networks.

There are also many subscription trend-forecasting services available online, including Worth Global Style Network (WGSN), Trendstop, Promostyl, and PeclersParis. Subscription services online provide the same information to all subscribers, though many services offer customized reporting and analysis.

FASHION FOCUS FROM THE FIELD: WORTH GLOBAL STYLE NETWORK

In a crowded office in London, researchers and writers work at their computers to publish the Worth Global Style Network (WGSN) online business-to-business news and information service for the fashion and style industry. It currently offers over 300,000 pages of up-to-the-minute international style trends and information. A team of 200 international writers, photographers, researchers, analysts, and trendspotters gather and interpret everything relevant to style. The trend service works on behalf of the more than 35,000 subscribing designers, manufacturers, retailers, and marketing professionals to keep up with the constant changes that influence their businesses.

WGSN was established in 1998 and describes its role as one of developing creative intelligence. The company tracks innovation and inspiration, continually interpreting the information for its individual clients. It has also provided over 8,000 seminars for its industry clients. With over forty new stories a day, an image archive of 4.8 million, and 14,000 graphics to download it is a leader in online trend services. Unique features include sections such as Think Tank, City by City, Materials, Retail Talk, and Active Sports.

WGSN makes the site available at a reduced cost to schools for educational purposes. Of particular interest to students is the feature "Generation Now," which showcases the portfolios and shows of recent design graduates. It provides advice on preparing, working, and locating employment in the textile and apparel industry, along with footwear, jewelry, promotion, and marketing. With this service, WGSN is preparing the next generation of fashion professionals to develop high standards for information, inspiration, and analysis.

Though the Internet is the top research source, travel to visit cities and shows, suppliers and factories, museums and events has continued. Meeting people face to face; seeing garments on the runway, in exhibits, or in shops; touching fabrics; and observing production are still the richest sources of information because the experience is live. Pictures, sketches, swatches, clothing, objects, and art provide a very tangible, visual source of information. Personal observation also allows individual interpretation of the information that is not edited by an outside source.

While the Internet is viewed as a filtered source, it has equalized access to information for smaller companies that may not have the resources for travel or subscriptions to a trend-forecasting service. Designers have a responsibility to use valid and reliable sources that acknowledge the original source of the information, including permissions for images. Authors; URLs from .edu, .gov, and .org sources;

Figure 2.1 Coming Apart at the Seams: Style and Social Fabric of the 1920s exhibition, 1996, courtesy of the Goldstein Museum of Design.

and reputable magazines, journals, and news organizations are generally trustworthy. Critical or controversial information should always be validated. Credit should be given in any written or oral presentation, particularly for original design ideas. These are not just issues of concern in education but can have a lasting impact on a designer's reputation in the industry.

For a designer, the most critical part of research is not the gathering of information, images, and swatches of fabric but the interpretation of these elements. All companies and designers need to interpret the information in terms of how it relates to their own brand and customer. This includes appropriateness, price point, and stage in the fashion adoption cycle. If transparent fabrics play a large role in a trend toward texture, and my customer needs conservative work apparel, I may show a vest with my blouses or reserve the transparent fabric for a scarf. The wrinkle-resistant finish on a dress shirt may be a big selling point for those who do their own laundry, but it is a nonissue for those who send their shirts out to be cleaned and pressed.

Lifestyle

Knowing who your customers are and what type of lifestyle they lead is critical to developing a successful design. Lifestyle refers to the overall feelings and practices that influence the selection and use of all the products in an individual's life: from clothes to cars, and furniture to food. Designers cannot assume that they understand a group of individuals based on casual acquaintances or by projecting themselves into their customers' lives. Solid information from census data, consumer research sources, interviews, observations, sales data, and customer feedback can help build an accurate profile. The Internet can be a source for public information, but most of this very valuable information is proprietary, and each company will need to develop its own profiles based on in-house research or through consulting with a consumer research service.

Lifestyle is a view that allows designers to know their customers beyond stereotypes. It can be a currently lived lifestyle or one that is an aspiration. Lifestyle branding builds on consumers' concept of an ideal existence, regardless of the reality. For example, a new assistant designer may eat soup for dinner every night to save up money that will allow her to dress like the designer she aspires to be. Consumers prefer to think of themselves as individuals with unique needs and desires. Most do not want to be placed in a generalized group such as millennials or baby boomers, or based on age, race, gender, or income. Consumers have evolved into individual paradoxes that defy general group definitions. A woman could have a lifestyle that includes a professional job, an interest in motorcycles, no children, and responsibility for her aging parents. A lifestyle view would put this woman into several smaller niches, allowing an apparel company to address a specific element of her lifestyle such as motorcycle gear, which would not be met by the niche that dresses her for her job. Thus she would join other women who ride motorcycles as a small niche even though the others may be younger and have families or more income. This allows for more flexibility in the way we view consumers and demands more attention to the garments designed for a specific niche. It creates an opportunity for designers to really target the needs of those in the niche and let go of the idea that a single design or concept can satisfy all.

Inspiration

Designers search for inspiration in the world around them. You may have heard a designer being asked, "What was your inspiration for this line?" Answers vary widely, but the source of inspiration is usually a motivating factor for the designer that provides a concept and visual direction. There is often some connection between the inspiration and the customer but not always.

Fashion reflects the time period in which it is designed and first worn. Anatole France, a Nobel laureate in 1921, wrote,

> If I were allowed to choose from the pile of books which will be published one hundred years after my death, do you know which one I would take? I would simply take a fashion magazine so that I could see how women dress one century after my departure. And these rags would tell me more about humanity of the future than all the philosophers, novelists, prophets and scholars. (Brousson, 1925, 156; translated by J. Pollock)

Current events, then, provide a huge source of inspiration for designers. Politics, the economy, war, movies, music, art, and books have been and will continue to be sources of inspiration. During women's struggle for equality in the workplace in the 1970s, women's work fashions were patterned after traditional menswear. The navy blue skirted suit with a white blouse and soft paisley bow tie was a familiar uniform that expressed this struggle. In the early twenty-first century, women in the workplace have more confidence and power, thus are dressing to express their feminine strengths. The movie *Flashdance* introduced a period of ripped and cut exercise wear along with leg warmers and bodysuits during a time when exercise was gaining popularity. Grunge music inspired grunge fashion in the early 1990s, and Karl Lagerfeld for Chanel borrowed from rappers' dress when he showed big chains and bling on the Paris runway. Sometimes an individual becomes an inspiration either as a public figure or a personal muse. Audrey Hepburn continues to be an inspiration for many designers, and Madonna was Jean Paul Gaultier's muse during the 1980s and 1990s. Sofia Coppola is muse to Marc Jacobs as she characterizes his vision of the sweet, young, innocent girl.

Sports are a huge inspiration. Tennis, golf, swimming, horse riding, and skiing apparel and clothing inspired by sports have become a big part of our everyday dress. Polo-style shirts, tennis shoes, and ski jackets are common items of dress in the Western world. Active sports and the concept of separates and casual dress provided the foundation for American sportswear. The game of polo became the successful inspiration for Ralph Lauren, and Narciso Rodriguez uses sports-inspired details in his designs. High-performance sportswear that originated in the Olympics or professional sports often trickles down and becomes part of our everyday wear. Wicking fabrics, seamless knits, and high-performance shoes are worn as fashion in addition to their use for active sports.

Travel is a rewarding source of inspiration that can serve to change views and perspectives. Exposure to a new place, culture, or experience can inspire a designer visually and offer a fresh approach to designing. Travel also allows the opportunity to search and shop markets for local handmade fabrics, jewelry, and crafts; explore flea markets and antique stalls; visit galleries; and, perhaps best of all, people watch. A few of the best-known spots to explore include Portobello Road in London, Les Puces de Saint-Ouen in Paris, Dongdaemun market in Seoul, the Rose Bowl Flea Market in Los Angeles, and Annex/Hell's Kitchen Flea Market in New York, but great markets can be found most anywhere. A sketchbook and camera to record observations are key to saving found inspirations. Polite requests for personal pictures or for shots in museums or galleries and discreet sketching are the most respectful way to gather these ideas. Photography in public places is generally allowed, but be aware of local cultures and traditions that may prohibit pictures.

A common yet endlessly amazing inspiration is nature. Whether experienced live or through various media, the beauty of form, color, and texture creates an emotional response. Even the harsher side of nature can provide points of reflection that can inspire. Looking more deeply at the evolution of a species as it has adapted to its environments is a rich source of ideas referred to as biomimicry. For example, designers can learn how to improve the speed of a swimmer by developing garments that mimic different properties of fish that allow them to move quickly.

Many designers look to fabric for their inspiration. The visual elements of color, texture, pattern, and drape attract the eye, but the tactile qualities of a textile often provide the greatest allure. A designer will touch and fold, gather and drape, and carry the fabric around to lay it against other fabrics or look at it in different light or from a distance. This is the medium of fashion, and it can make the imagination race.

Textile trade shows are important destinations for designers so they can select the season's fabrics from a variety of vendors. Direction, INTERCOT, Interstoff, the Intex trade fair in India, and Fabric at MAGIC are well-known international exhibits. Premiere Vision is an international show exhibiting in Paris, New York,

Figure 2.2 Portobello Road flea market, 2005, London, photographer Adrian Pingstone.

Figure 2.3 Dongdaemun market, 2006, courtesy of E. Bye.

Moscow, and Shanghai. Many countries with a large textile or apparel industry hold some form of textile exhibition, each with its own specialties. These events are not open to the public, and registration as a designer or wholesale business is required for entry.

Designers can also visit local showrooms to review fabrics, or a sales representative can bring samples to the studio. Some designers are very involved in developing exclusive fabrics for their designs and work with textile mills and textile printers to develop original ideas. Lead time and costs are generally higher with this process. However, developing unique fabrics and prints can deliver added value to the consumer in terms of both aesthetics and performance, setting the garments apart from others available in the market.

FASHION FOCUS FROM THE FIELD: INDIAN EMBROIDERY

Janell Berté is a bridal wear designer who has used embroidery sourced from India on her gowns. India is well known for its expertise in and tradition of hand-embellished fabrics. Designers can work directly with a factory or through an agency that supplies design and manufacturing services to develop custom embroidery. An agency can be an advantage for a smaller designer because it provides design services and handles all the interactions with the factories including the final import and customs requirements. Working directly with a factory can be a cost savings; however, it requires much more time to develop the designs and oversee the development of the embroidery.

Figure 2.4 Janell Berté wedding gown embroidered by Indian artisans, 2008, courtesy of Janell Berté, photographer Chris Knight.

Berté recommends building a relationship with someone you trust for both agency and direct approaches. Ethical practices cannot be assumed, and copying of designs does occur. Without government regulations, trust is the best protection. The quality of the embroidery is generally high, so in addition to ethics, a designer must consider the manufacturer's aesthetic style. The style strongly influences the interpretation of original designs, so it is important to find one that complements the desired results and to request approval samples. Samples are developed from a garment pattern (for example, a bodice) that includes a detailed drawing of the embroidery in the exact location. A key is developed to identify each type of thread, stitch, and bead. The completed piece is then returned for final cutting and manufacturing. This takes careful planning and a high level of expertise.

New fibers, finishes, and fabrics enter the market regularly. Companies often enter promotional agreements with designers who agree to use the new textile in their line or to design garments for promoting the new textile. Designers are interested in new textile technologies as they can provide opportunities for new aesthetics, comfort, and performance. New construction techniques, such as seam welding, often need to be developed. The results not only impact the aesthetic of the garment but also introduce new manufacturing methods. Willingness to experiment and an understanding of what the customer is willing to wear guide the adoption of a new textile. Gradual change is more easily accepted than radical change. For example, spandex was gradually introduced in active sportswear and then moved into jeans and casual clothing. Today it is even in demand for our professional garments. A more in-depth discussion of new textile technologies is presented in chapter 7.

Technological influences on fashion design

Fashion's reputation for rapid change and forward thinking is in part due to advances in science and technology. The fields of chemistry, computer science, aerospace engineering, automotive engineering, architecture, industrial textiles, and competitive athletic wear are reflected in the clothing we wear everyday and have had a big impact on the way we design and produce clothing.

Historical technological innovations such as the development of the sewing machine, the zipper, and synthetic fibers have influenced how garments are made, how they look, and how they perform. Elsa Schiaparelli experimented with synthetic fibers when they were new and introduced the first zipper to Paris couture, establishing a sleek fashion silhouette. Andre Courreges's use of bonded jersey, Pierre Cardin's pioneering vacuum-formed fabrics, and Issey Miyake's pleats began to push the boundaries of fashion through experimentation with technology and innovative materials. Hussein Chalayan and Nicolas Ghesquière are current leaders in experimentation with new technology for apparel. See chapter 7 for further discussion.

The internet and global communication systems

The Internet has changed the way we communicate, retrieve information, and conduct business. Most of us cannot imagine what our life would be like without computers and cell phones. Investments in communication research by the U.S. government and military laid the foundation for the Internet in the 1960s. The commercialization of Internet service providers in the 1980s led to the growth of the World Wide Web (Web) and to e-mail in the 1990s. This was truly a change in paradigm for businesses and individuals.

Search engines can bring information, images, and sound directly to our desks in an instant. Communicating, shopping, banking, telecommuting, listening to music, and watching videos digitally are common practices in our lives, and opportunities continue to expand. The need to develop new laws and safeguards for electronic communication has also expanded, along with the need to establish ethical practices. Rapid communication and new methods of doing business have allowed an increase in the speed at which fashion is produced, thus allowing fashion to change more easily and frequently. Few people have questioned the impact of these rapid changes, but perhaps they deserve review.

Designers can conduct their research and hold meetings without traveling, can send images and specifications to colleagues and vendors around the world, and can source and sell products electronically. Employees around the world can be working 24/7 on a project, taking advantage of their global resources. Less travel, more accurate and immediate information, and rapid turnaround that allows a constant flow of resources have reduced costs and improved the quality of apparel. Instant access to information has also increased the awareness and demands of consumers and increased competition.

Designers and their teams need to be aware that too much information can be overwhelming. At times it is necessary to limit exposure to information and inspiration in order to focus attention and prioritize projects. Designers need to protect themselves, as creativity requires quiet, reflective periods of time to let the mind wander and allow new connections to form.

Computer-aided design

The last quarter of the twentieth century saw rapid development of computer technology. Computer-aided design (CAD) and computer-aided manufacturing (CAM) dramatically changed the process of designing and manufacturing garments by reducing many labor-intensive processes, increasing speed and accuracy, and lowering costs. Garments can be developed with CAD/CAM from sketch to pattern and cutting, either locally or globally, in a fraction of the time it took twenty-five years ago.

Many designers spend the majority of their day researching, developing concepts and designs, and preparing electronic presentations using some type of CAD software. Designers can use a variety of specialized or off-the-shelf software to sketch, color, and present design concepts. They can sketch with a pencil-like tool, scan images or textiles, or download images from the Internet. Apparel industry software and equipment producers include Gerber, Lectra, and Optitex, while Adobe offers CD5 Photoshop and Illustrator off-the-shelf. Features that support the way a designer works, ease of learning and use, and cost are considered when selecting a software package. Current designers expect to learn new software approximately every four years in addition to keeping up with their regular responsibilities.

FASHION FOCUS FROM THE FIELD: HMX SPORTSWEAR

HMX Sportswear, a private subsidiary of Hartmarx that manufactures sportswear for men and women, believes that the foundation of a successful fashion company is great design. They focus on developing innovative luxury products and use technology to streamline product-development cycles. The designers at HMX use a commercial software package that combines presentation, drawing, and original fabric development. This one platform allows designers to work and communicate more efficiently and smoothly, allowing more time for creativity. The system is flexible. Designers can experiment with different ideas and techniques to make revisions quickly. Style lines, details, and colors can be changed quickly, and the results are visible immediately. Variations can be saved for later evaluation, and the number of samples that must be made is reduced. This accelerates the product-development process, saving time and costs.

HMX designers use CAD presentation boards to communicate the line and collection concepts. They value the clean images and feel that they represent the garments more accurately. The images transfer seamlessly to their business software, making overall company communication more efficient. Planning, merchandising, and manufacturing also realize improvements in cost and productivity as a result of starting the design process using robust design technology.

CAD software for patternmaking, grading, and marker making is well established in the industry. The speed and accuracy of the software are invaluable when used by an experienced designer or patternmaker. The ability to easily store and retrieve previously used patterns, grade rules, and markers facilitates the repetitive parts of the task, allowing energy to be used on creative design and problem solving. Patterns and markers can be engineered to achieve better fabric utilization, thus reducing costs. Grading can be customized for a unique size range or custom fit requirements. Patterns and markers are able to be sent electronically to a vendor or automatic cutter anywhere in the world, allowing flexibility for human resources. The designer can work in New York while the patternmaker lives and works in Los Angeles, and the cutting and sewing can be done in Taiwan. Sewing is the one operation that has been challenging to computerize, and it continues to rely heavily on skilled operators.

New software is available that allows design and patternmaking to occur in three dimensions. Patterns can be draped or input digitally and then joined and fitted on a 3-D avatar, a digital representation of the body. The 3-D avatar can be created according to individual body measurements, or a body scan of a real person can be used as the avatar fit model. This speeds the process of fitting a garment and revising the patterns, thus reducing the need for numerous sample revisions. Tukatech has adapted its e-fit software for iPhone compatibility, making the fit session mobile. This 3-D technology also provides new opportunities for virtual fashion shows, virtual stores, and virtual dressing rooms. Real samples are still necessary to evaluate fabric quality, construction, and dynamic fit.

The cost of these CAD systems has been greatly reduced with the introduction of the personal computer. The return on investment is usually less than one year, making these systems affordable for both large and small companies. For those who do not want to invest in their own CAD system, some cities have businesses that offer a central service site with CAD equipment and software that can be rented by the hour. This is a great cost-saving advantage for new designers and smaller businesses. Training is available in addition to consulting services. This business model also allows more frequent updates of the software as the costs are shared by many individual designers.

Technology is also used to control and track garments during production, and to keep track of inventory and distribution. Many companies use product-development-management software to organize and track all the records of an individual garment from concept to delivery, including images. Multiple people can view and work on the record, easing the paperwork needed for production and delivery, which often occurs internationally. This software is available from apparel industry CAD companies but is often developed by the individual apparel company to better meet its unique needs.

In theory, a garment could be researched, designed, patterned, graded, and test fitted without the use of any paper or fabric! However, most designers and companies still find it essential to print, plot, and create their work in a tangible form. The separation of the designer from production creates challenges in communication and understanding for everyone. Strong integration between design and production is essential for a successful, high-quality, cost-effective garment. Unfortunately this is often the weakest link, and many designers do not have a good understanding of what happens during production or how their decisions impact that part of the process.

There is also a countertrend to our increasing use of technology. Mass-produced apparel is often negatively viewed as uniform, despite the quality and value that technology has provided. A growing desire for individuality and balance is supported by the trend to include an indication of the hand or person that created the garment. Thus imperfection becomes desirable in contrast to the uniformity and quality that can be achieved with technology. Many companies are working to find the right balance between local, domestic, and offshore production that can support the quality and value that they need to stay in business. Another version of this are the Japanese designers Rei Kawakubo, Issey Miyake, Yohji Yamamoto, Junya Watanabe, and Michiko Koshino, who have been leaders in combining traditional craft techniques with cutting-edge technology. They value looking back and looking forward. The growing craft trend, including knitting, scrapbooking, and making jewelry, is in response to a high level of technology use in Western society. More hand detailing in the form of embroidery, beading, and appliqué is evident in many designers' recent lines. The look of handwork is popular on mass-produced items, though the production is usually done by machine.

FASHION FOCUS FROM THE FIELD: ANN TAYLOR LOFT

Ann Taylor Loft designs updated classics for the value-conscious woman with a relaxed lifestyle. The designers are in touch with what their client wants: a feminine, stylish, versatile wardrobe. Apparel is developed using much the same processes as other retail manufacturers, with an unusual twist. The design leaders at the company have embraced the positive qualities of hand-done presentations. These include development sketches, illustrations, formal presentations, and technical sketches. CAD is not part of the process. The style and attitude that are expressed by hand are highly valued. The images convey a sense of movement unlike the often-rigid sketches produced using CAD. They feel that it is easier to convey proportions, make decisions during development, and convey the final concept when the sketches are rendered by hand. This is more labor-intensive, and freelance illustrators are often used, but the tactile qualities captured in their visual presentations accurately represent the brand.

Investments are made in new designers, who are mentored to develop their hand-drawing skills. Great professional pride is taken as a new designer sees these skills improving. This appreciation of hands-on processes is also seen in their draping room, where a design can be developed or experiments done with mock samples. A fabric flower might be shaped, layouts of beading and trim created, or sweater patterns tested. Working back and forth from 3-D to 2-D generates accurate, realistic designs. For Ann Taylor Loft, the quality of the work takes priority over speed.

Line concept

Developing the line concept is critical to the success of the line. It provides the direction or plan for all the work that follows the initial research. It must also help the company reach its business goals. The designer, often in conjunction with the merchandiser, reviews the research and past business reports to determine a theme, silhouette, and color story along with a target assortment that will yield the desired profits. A line includes the total range of garments that will be offered during a season. Some new designers start with lines of eight to ten pieces while large companies can have multiple groups in a line totaling several hundred pieces. The number and variety of individual styles and groups of garments are determined by considering the desired depth and breadth of the assortment. Parameters are set around cost, style, color, and type of garment. For example, a simple line may consist of two pants, one skirt, one dress, two jackets, and three tops to be offered in two colorways, using two solid and one printed fabrication for each. Within these parameters, the designer can begin to develop ideas for the line. The business plan guides the designer by setting a focus and specific goals.

The development of creative ideas for the line can be challenging under set business parameters, but it is essential to maintain the focus on the brand and customer. It is also important for most companies to maintain a sense of evolution from the previous season. While consumers are generally looking for something new, they are more likely to accept change when it occurs gradually and is related to something they are currently wearing. Designers must consider a multitude of variables to predict the future, unspoken desires of the consumer. Change in fashion is not the sole responsibility of the designer but also requires the support of the broader industry, including the fashion press, and ultimately of the individual making the purchase. Ian Griffiths expresses the magnitude of this challenge in this quote: "The most innovative and inspired clothes on earth are products to be bought and worn. They are not art, but no less worthy for not being so: if only there was an opposite critical structure in which to locate their triumph" (2000, p. 83).

Original designs take the most time to develop and require sketching many more ideas than will actually be used. The sketches are reviewed, and 100 ideas may be pared down to 30 that will be made into samples. Frequently, a designer works from designs that were strong sellers during a previous season. Modifying a style by changing the details, the color, or the fabrication can reduce the time and cost of developing garments for a new line. Last season's jacket may get a different fabrication, a change to welt pockets, and new buttons. A third but more controversial method is the use of knockoffs. Companies operating at lower price points often copy garments they have purchased or images from magazines or the Internet. The style and proportion are generally copied directly, while the color and fabrications are changed. At this price point, it is often necessary to greatly reduce development costs and generally not necessary to be ahead in the fashion cycle. The practice of knocking off a design is common in the industry because current copyright laws do not protect garment designs. Textile prints, because of their graphic qualities, are more easily protected. There is growing concern about this practice, but until legal protection is enacted designers will need to practice ethical judgment on their own. See further discussion in chapter 4.

Figure 2.5 Sample of designer's ideation book, 2005, courtesy of Allison Quinnell, photographer E. Bye.

All the proposed designs, regardless of their origins, are presented on a designer workboard as a flat sketch. The ideas are reviewed for their individual strengths, their relationship to the line concept, and their estimated cost. An open, objective critique is essential to pull together a strong line. The review is focused on the designs, and the criteria set for their evaluation are taken from the original line concept and business plan. The critique is not about the designer, and personal attachment to a design must be dismissed. The review process can take several iterations to identify the garments for each group within the line. Often there will be missing pieces, so further design ideation is necessary. Revisions due to cost are frequent. Fabric and labor costs must be balanced to achieve the desired price point. A full skirt may require less expensive fabric or a reduction in the amount of fabric that is needed to meet the established sale price. If a solution cannot be found, the garment is usually dropped from the line. The final selection of garments is made into samples for further review.

Before a pattern and sample can be developed, the garment's technical and trim details must be decided. This is done by the designer, or in larger companies it becomes the responsibility of a technical designer. The details of the garment must be clearly conceptualized. These include the final fabric, understructure, closure types, trims and

Figure 2.6 Sample of industry line board, 2008, courtesy of Elyse Olson.

accessories, edge finishes, seam and stitch types, labeling, tags, and packaging. Size specifications are developed prior to vendor development, while garment measurements should be established after final approval.

The final fabric must be considered before a pattern is made. The structure (usually woven or knit), weight, drape, nap, or surface pattern guides each proceeding decision. The understructure such as interfacing or shoulder pads is a factor in the appearance and wear of a garment. Buttons or zippers, hooks or ties must be selected for compatibility and require specific patterning. This is also true for trims such as lace or piping and accessories such as belts or appliqués. Edge finishes such as binding on the neckline or a faced hem are determined based on the fabric, design, and cost. Seams and stitch types are selected based on fabric, performance, cost, and availability of equipment. Care and content labeling is required by law. Brand labeling is part of the total image of the brand along with any marketing or informational hangtags. Packaging is also a consideration. The final display methods for folded garments need to be taken into consideration, and garments on hangers often require internal hanging straps or a special hanger.

Designers must think ahead when selecting a fabric as it contributes the most to the final cost and also has the most impact on the garments' look, performance, and production. For example, the selection of a plaid fabric requires the designer to determine how important it is to match the plaid. Matching requires more fabric and is more challenging to cut and sew. This contributes to a higher cost; however, matched plaids are more visually pleasing and are considered a sign of quality. This may be important to your customer or of little consideration, in which case it ceases to be a design decision. Some alternatives may be to match the plaid only on the front of the garment

Figure 2.7 Hand marker making and cutting, 2004, courtesy of E. Bye.

where it is most noticeable, cut the garment on the bias (which also requires more fabric!), or perhaps balance the cost by removing the lining or a pocket or a belt.

Sample development

Samples are developed in a variety of ways depending on the individual company, but the basic process is the same. Many companies make their own samples, with designers working in close contact with the sample makers. Other companies send out the designs and develop specifications for a vendor to complete the sample-making process.

Once the sketch has been approved, the first patternmaker develops a pattern. The garment is cut, and then sewn by a sample maker. The sample maker needs a wide range of skills and knowledge as she will complete construction of the entire garment. It is not made on a production line. Her knowledge and skill are invaluable to the patternmaker and the designer as she can identify problems and offer solutions as the garment is developed.

Once the samples are complete, a fit session is held to evaluate the design and the fit of the garment on a fit model. Vendor-prepared samples are usually measured against the specifications that were sent with the sample request. These are the exact dimensions of the garment at specific locations such as the waist or sleeve length. The garment must be within a specified tolerance, for example, 0.25 inch, before it is put on a fit model. Meeting the specifications does not guarantee that the garment will fit as the designer intended. The fit session is attended by everyone involved in the development and production of the line including those in design, merchandising, patternmaking, technical design, production, and costing.

The garment is evaluated and approved, or suggestions are made to improve the garment's fit, look, or production. The model is asked to move around and give a personal report on the fit and comfort of the garment. Everyone is able to ask questions or point out potential problems that could affect the production and successful sale of the garment. Few garments are approved on the first review, though this is the goal because costs are greatly reduced. Most samples must go through more than one revision until approval is reached. Clear communication is critical so that revisions are easily understood by the people completing the pattern or production corrections whether they are in the next room or in another country.

Technology is being developed that has the potential to reduce the development time for an approved sample. Illustrations can be rendered in 3-D to allow better evaluation of the look of the garment in terms of proportions, silhouette, details, and color. 3-D body scanners are helping researchers develop sizing systems to improve fit for a wider range of body types. CAD patterns can be digitally placed onto a 3-D digital avatar, giving information regarding fit without ever needing a garment to be cut and sewn. Fabric type and weight can be programmed to give a good representation of the drape.

Textile and color approval

As the garment sample is developed, textile and color approval occurs simultaneously. As textiles are sourced, the samples must meet basic requirements. Some standards are mandated by the government including fiber and care labeling, flammability, and hazardous chemicals. Quality and performance standards set by the company can include minimum levels for colorfastness, shrinkage, strength, pilling, and abrasion. Special features such as wicking properties, insulation value, or stain resistance are tested before the feature is included on a hangtag.

Color management ensures that the consumer will be satisfied with colors that match in a line of clothing and provides a way to communicate that color information during development and production. Color definitions are organized using either the Scotdic Textile Color System based on the Munsell system or the Pantone Matching System. Both systems define clear numeric specifications that can be easily communicated. One of the challenges in garment production is to make sure that the colors in a line match regardless of the fiber or fabrication of the textile. Consumers want to be able to purchase a sweater knit from wool and a skirt woven in acrylic that match, regardless of the source. Lab dips of each color and fabrication are tested with a spectrophotometer and the human eye. A lab dip is a sample of the fabric that has been dyed. It can be challenging and time-consuming for the dye lab to achieve approval of the lab dips due to variables in the fiber, fabrication, finishes, chemicals, and environmental conditions. Lab-dip approval is initiated as early as possible during the development phase because final approval is required before production can begin.

Preproduction

Once the final line has been approved, several steps remain before a garment is ready for production. If the line is to be sold wholesale, sales samples must be made and distributed to the sales representatives. Final production depends on the number of orders that are taken. The merchandisers and buyers from companies whose product goes directly to their retail outlets must finalize their sales predictions to create an accurate order. Garments can be dropped from the line due to low orders.

Production patterns are made for those garments with profit-generating orders. A production pattern is engineered to exact size and style specifications and modified according to the final fabrication and equipment that will be used. For example, a pattern may need to be adjusted for expected shrinkage or for a special seam type. The finished pattern is then graded from the sample size to include patterns for each size in which the garment will be offered. Misses sizes 4–16, or 32–44, are common ranges. Markers are then made for each fabric type that will be cut, and these are designed to yield good fabric utilization. Markers provide the exact layout of the pattern pieces that need to be cut. Parameters can be set to control placement according to grain, nap, or matching. Some companies use CAD to develop their patterns, and most use CAD to grade patterns and develop markers. The markers are then cut by hand or with an automatic cutter that is guided by electronic data from the marker. Preproduction and production activities are frequently sourced through a vendor or contract manufacturer if there are no company-owned production facilities.

In tandem with the preproduction activities, specifications for the garments and all materials must be finalized. Orders for fabrics and materials must be placed so that they arrive in time for production schedules to be met. Quality-control inspections take place at the production site, and garments are shipped directly to distribution centers or retailers.

Each individual involved with the development, production, and marketing of an apparel line needs to be innovative and have a positive attitude. Ideas for improvements or new perspectives can come from anyone. While the designer may begin the process, those who produce, market, and merchandise the line are invested in it as well. Small changes can have an unanticipated chain reaction that affects the whole team both positively or negatively. The cutter who notices repeated flaws in the fabric before the cut begins can prevent an expensive error. The marker maker who notices that adding a center back seam can improve fabric utilization by 2 percent can reduce costs only if the designer approves the change. The sewer who continually experiences thread breakage on a new fabric needs help from an experienced production manager or the vendor who provided the fabric. If it was the designer who initiated the original fabric change, she needs to be aware of the impact it had on production and develop the foresight to avoid similar problems in the future.

The cycle begins again, with the results from the past season informing decisions to be made in the current season. Most companies produce two lines a year, spring/summer and fall/winter, with a few who may add a holiday or resort season. In order to drive sales, some companies offer an almost continuous production of new styles. These fast-fashion models adhere to a much shorter time frame for development and production, in part enabled by technology.

Summary

- To create more design opportunities, look at trends from the perspective of what's important, not just what's next.
- Countertrends occur in response to mainstream trends and provide insight into special niches.
- Research on the Internet or a live experience provides valuable information, but it is the interpretation of that information for the brand and customer that is critical.
- Lifestyle is a view that allows designers to target consumers' individual needs, letting go of the idea that a single design or concept can satisfy all.

- Inspiration is a motivating factor for the designer that provides a concept and visual direction found in the world around us.
- Fashion's reputation for rapid change and forward thinking is due to advances in science and technology.
- Rapid communication and new methods of doing business on the Internet have allowed an increase in the speed at which fashion is produced, thus allowing fashion to change more easily and frequently.
- CAD/CAM have dramatically changed, and will continue to change, the process of designing and manufacturing garments by reducing labor-intensive processes, increasing speed and accuracy, and lowering costs.
- The countertrend to the increased use of technology is the desire for products that reveal the touch of the human hand.
- The line concept in conjunction with the business plan guides the designer's work by setting a focus and specific goals.
- Sample development is the process of making a garment that is reviewed and revised for final approval and production.
- Textile and color approval ensures compliance with government regulations and customer satisfaction with color and performance.

Vocabulary

- avatar
- colorway
- countertrend
- fabrication
- grade rules
- lifestyle
- lead time
- markers
- niche
- trend

Discussion

1. Identify current trends in fashion and trace their origin to a broader trend or countertrend.
2. What resources are available in your city for research and inspiration?
3. Review the current lines of several designers to determine their inspiration. How does the inspiration connect to the brand and customer?
4. Identify and describe several niches for apparel.
5. Debate the pros and cons of using knockoffs.
6. Compare a couture garment and a mass-produced garment and evaluate the use of technology on each.
7. Select a mass-produced garment at a higher price point. How would you redesign it to lower the price point while maintaining the look?
8. What are the positive and negative consequences of the technology used to produce apparel?
9. Discuss some of the ethical decisions that may arise for a designer.
10. What decision would you make in the following scenarios?

a The lab dips have not been approved, but if production doesn't start tomorrow you will ship late and risk a 20 percent penalty from the retailer. It is an order that contributes 30 percent to your bottom line.

b A skirt is included in your fall catalog, but the sample is on its fourth revision and will likely not be ready for shipping when the catalog comes out. A matching blouse has already been approved and production has started. It is a beautiful bias-cut skirt with a dramatic drape, but the samples keep coming back with an uneven hem.

c The denim that you selected did not pass the color crocking test, so a less-than-ideal substitution was made and the fabric ordered. You just received a call from the fabric representative telling you that a new dye lot of the original fabric has been tested that meets the color crocking requirements. The patterns and markers are complete but have not been cut due to a problem with the automatic cutter. The original fabric had a nap while the substitution does not. If you decide to use the original fabric with the new dye lot, what impact could this have on production?

3

DESIGNER PRACTICES

There are multiple ways that fashion designers work, and their specific responsibilities can vary greatly. The depth and breadth of these various designer roles depend on the goals of the business and how it is organized. A slightly different set of knowledge and skills, along with unique personal strengths, is required for each role. Designers need strong creative and technical skills including construction, patternmaking, and sketching. The ability to interpret trends for a specific consumer based on original or published research is fundamental to being a designer. A good understanding of how a business operates and maintaining a sense of the current business climate are also important. The ability to present and sell your design ideas is invaluable, and as in any business, good communication skills and teamwork are essential. Designers should be able to analyze the needs of the consumer and translate them to a product; generate a variety of original concepts; vision future possibilities; discover new ways to address change in the market, the environment, or materials; and coordinate actions and activities that meet company objectives. Some designers learn that they enjoy the entire process from concept to sale, while others discover that their strength lies in one facet of the process such as research, sketching, or draping.

Fashion design is a creative field, and there is high competition for the best jobs. The majority of opportunities are with companies that design clothing for the mass market, because this is where there is the greatest number of consumers. While this area of the industry may not seem as creative or glamorous as the high-end and luxury market, there are some real benefits. Creativity is truly tested when designing under strict financial constraints; successful designers will see their designs in stores, online, and being worn by numerous people; there is greater potential to really influence how the majority of society dresses; and these companies typically provide strong salary and benefits packages, opportunities for professional development, and room to advance a career at the same company. Leadership skills can help many designers advance to positions in management including chief designer, design director, or president.

Positions in high fashion are extremely competitive because the market is considerably smaller and the investment to build and maintain the companies is large.

For those who want to pursue a career in high fashion, the reality is that typical starting salaries are lower than those with mass-market companies, and the odds of becoming the next Vera Wang or Marc Jacobs are roughly 160,000:1 (The Princeton Review, 2008). Designers who are entrepreneurs or work freelance typically have the lowest income, though a successful entrepreneur has the potential to make many times what a salaried designer earns. Most design positions are located in large fashion cities or regional fashion centers, but opportunities also exist in smaller, less central cities and regions.

All designers should expect to work long hours with an often irregular schedule. This will vary depending on individual responsibilities, amount of travel, and what stage of the development and production cycle is occurring. For example, preparing for market, a show, or a delivery date can send everyone into an intense period of work. Time, financial, and customer constraints are a constant because ultimately the designer supports a business. Dedication, drive, and innovation are qualities that are paramount for a successful design career. Many designers describe their "passion for fashion," and though this is a cliché there does seem to be some inner force that can only be satisfied by designing. Most designers cannot imagine doing anything else, and in the end it is a good thing to love what you do.

There are many opportunities for designers that go beyond designing apparel. These might include positions with support industries such as textile or trim companies, color forecasting, training others to use new software or equipment, sales, marketing, journalism, events coordinators, and others. With experience, continuing education, and some self-reflection, most designers find their niche in the apparel industry. This chapter takes the basic process of developing a line from chapter 2 and presents variations to the role of designer.

Vendor

The role of a designer who works directly for a vendor is to provide services for clients who have hired the vendor to produce an order of garments. The designer is part of the team that ensures that the requests and specifications from the client are executed satisfactorily. When the order arrives, the designer reviews the materials and initiates the process. The designer may drape or pattern the first sample or work with a patternmaker on the team. The sample is constructed with the designer taking the role of problem solver with issues that arise in the development of the sample. The sample is checked against the specifications and then sent to the client for approval, with revisions as needed.

Some vendors offer full design services including research and development, depending on the clients' needs. This type of request usually comes from business entrepreneurs with little background or experience in apparel design and manufacturing. Vendor designers may develop private-label lines under contract from a client. The clients, often retailers, contract for specific garments or lines to be

Figure 3.1 Developing a garment through draping, 2007, courtesy of Anna Carlson.

developed under their guidelines and directions. The retailer often collaborates in the conceptual development of the design but does not execute any of the design work. This can occur if the retailer does not have the capacity to do the design work, or it may be a unique product that the retailer does not want to develop due to time or cost constraints. For example, a special line of holiday sweaters might require the unique skills of a knitwear designer and sourcing of unusual yarns that go beyond the retailer's in-house resources.

An alternate and more common option is for the vendor designer to develop a line for a private-label retailer in response to a bid request. Samples are developed according to the bid request and then presented to the retail buyers, usually in a competitive situation. The buyers make a selection and then place an order. These efforts to acquire new clients and business are often critical to a vendor's success. Production is the core business for the vendor; however, a strong designer plays an important role in winning bids that keep the factory in operation. It is generally considered good business practice to limit the work accepted from any one client to approximately 50 percent of capacity. The clients must also try to balance their contracts between vendors. This provides some level of protection that the vendor will still be in business if a contract is canceled or that store shelves will not be empty if the vendor is unable to deliver.

Currently, most designers who work for a vendor work at, or close to, the factory. The locations are primarily international, though some domestic production is still in operation. International positions require strong communication skills and fluency in a second language. This is a service position so the ability to work under time constraints and interpret the needs of the client is essential.

Private-label retailer

There has been a dramatic increase in the sale of private-label garments for retailers, and they currently make up over 35 percent of the assortment in some retail stores. The main reason is a better bottom line. Garments are manufactured through vendors, and the products are delivered directly to the retailer. This eliminates any wholesale markups. Retailers also have more control over how garments are displayed and advertised. Many retailers still carry brand-name apparel, but the proportion of private-label merchandise is continuing to rise.

The designer for a private-label retailer directs business to many vendors. The designer in this role is responsible for developing private-label lines for the retailer that will be sold only in its own retail outlets. With the goal of providing exclusive products that meet the customers' needs, the designer is able to focus research and development in a very specific direction. This designer follows the development process from research through line approval (see chapter 2), most often as part of a team. Other responsibilities include presentations to buyers, merchandisers, and upper-level management to introduce line concepts, and collaboration to establish the final pieces in the collection. Specifications and vendor packs with all the essential information regarding each garment are prepared by a technical design team or an assistant designer. These include technical flats, sizing, materials and trims, stitches, color specifications, and costing goals. The pack is sent to the vendor and the sample returned. The technical design team prepares the sample for a fit evaluation where the designer and other members of the evaluation team can review both the technical and aesthetic aspects of the sample. The sample is either approved or requests for revision are prepared and sent to the vendor for another sample.

The designer is far removed from the manufacturing in this case, which can make communication difficult. Trips to visit the vendor help to improve communication and understanding; however, international travel requires additional professional skills. A strong understanding of construction, materials, and production is an advantage for private-label designers. This designer needs to work well on a team and be organized and able to thrive in a more corporate, high-pressure environment. As designers gain experience, they are also in a position to train and mentor younger designers, so leadership and management skills grow in importance. A strong bottom line, along with the ability to demonstrate the values of the company, is an important indicator of a successful private-label designer. Though these design positions are often demanding and stressful, they usually offer more security in the form of higher salary, benefits, and professional development.

Brand-label business

Brand labels are nationally or internationally recognized and support the image of a particular company. Burberry, Levi's, and Coach are well-known brands developed by a team of designers with a head designer or design director providing leadership and vision. Brand-label garments can be purchased wholesale by a retailer for resale, or they may be sold in an independent boutique located in a larger retail store or in brand-name stores. The designer in this role is responsible for developing the lines that will be sold internationally through a variety of retail outlets. The main objective is to strengthen the brand image, remaining true to the history of the brand while still looking forward. The designer must be able to recognize, capture, and translate the brand in every garment. The goal is to evolve the brand; thus this designer has a very specific goal that must support the marketing and image determined by the company leaders. This designer follows the development process from research through line approval (see chapter 2) and may be involved with the marketing and visual merchandising of the products.

The level of designer involvement with manufacturing depends on the factory and the individual company. Some companies have their own manufacturing facilities where it is easier for the designer to keep a close eye on the garments. Communication and operations are greatly eased as all are part of the same company with the same goals. A few companies operate as vertical manufacturers, which gives them more control over the entire process. This is when one manufacturer is responsible for every step of producing the garment, from fiber and fabric to sewing and distribution. Other brand-label companies use a vendor to manufacture their garments and operate in a similar fashion to private-label retailers.

The brand-label designer needs to work well on a team and be organized and able to be creative within the parameters of the brand. This designer approaches the market from the perspective of a wholesaler: In addition to responding to the needs of the final consumer, the line must also appeal to the retail buyer. Cost is more critical in this situation because the retailer will usually mark up the wholesale price by 50 percent for the consumer. Many samples are never manufactured because orders are not sufficient for a wholesale profit. Thus, much of the designer's work is never sold and worn. Most brand-name designers are anonymous to the public as the goal is to promote the brand, not the name of the designer.

Freelance designer

A freelance designer can be responsible for all or part of the development process based on the needs of the client. One client may require only research and sketches of proposed designs, while another may want delivery of the final approved sample. Sometimes a color or theme direction is provided, or it may be a more open assignment. Deliverables might include computer files or printouts, mock samples, boards, presentations, and specification sheets. Clients may be individuals, companies without their own design staff, or companies with design staff who are looking for temporary help or a new perspective.

A freelance designer is really an entrepreneur with all the advantages and challenges of owning a business. To get started, it is essential to have strong and varied

Figure 3.2 Freelance development materials, 2008, courtesy of E. Bye.

design experience and a wide network of professional contacts across the industry. This designer can pick and choose the type and number of jobs, and set the work schedule and prices. Payment can be arranged as a percentage of the final business, by the project, at an hourly rate, or as a salary. Benefits are typically not part of the arrangement but should be considered when determining overall costs.

The business and legal side of freelancing is critical to the security and success of a freelance designer. It may be necessary to hire services to support the business including an accountant who can handle billing and tax issues, a lawyer who can advise on contracts, or an insurance agent. The designer needs to do the research regarding what is required to operate a business, because the designer is ultimately responsible for the business and the design work. Clarifying expectations and deliverables with the client and using a contact can help to protect both parties from liability claims. Insurance for counterfeit protection is a smart decision in an environment of ethical uncertainty.

There is a greater sense of control with freelance work that holds strong appeal for many designers who have worked for established companies. Success as a freelance designer also requires discipline, good time management, and organization skills. Self-motivation and the ability to work well on your own are important personal qualities. Excellent communication skills for supporting the design work and negotiating are essential. Working under short deadlines, balancing busy stretches of time with downtimes, and continuing personal professional development can be challenging. Many freelance designers develop a support network of other freelance designers for professional feedback and connections, to pool resources and discuss trends and current issues.

FASHION FOCUS FROM THE FIELD: "SARAH," ANONYMOUS DESIGNER IN TRANSITION

Sarah is currently doing freelance design work in addition to developing her own line of textiles. She spent fifteen years in the apparel industry as a designer for a mass-market brand. Early in her career the work was exciting and she was learning a great deal. She felt well prepared with her bachelor's degree in fashion design, but there was a considerable amount of new things to learn. Being on a team, communicating with vendors, designing under customer and budget parameters, and meeting the fast pace were challenging. As she was promoted, the corporate atmosphere became more familiar. Sarah was comfortable using new software, and technology and travel became a growing part of her job. She developed strong leadership skills and the reputation for being a good designer. Slowly she started to feel that there were too many meetings and that the pace never slowed down: It was not a creative atmosphere, and she missed the hands-on component of designing. Sarah refers to this as burnout and reveals that many of her female peers were feeling the same. She had done well financially and had been smart about her savings, so she made a difficult decision to leave and try freelancing. She had experience and numerous contacts, so the risk was ultimately successful. While she wouldn't trade her experience as a designer for a corporate company, she values the creative control and variety in her new career.

Designer as manufacturer

The designer as manufacturer is responsible for the entire process from concept to the final sale and has more flexibility to quickly respond to changes in the market than a larger company. This designer is an individual who enjoys all parts of the process from research, patternmaking, cutting, and sewing to finishing, packaging, marketing, and sales. There is great variety in the day-to-day activities of this designer. The workdays and -weeks are long, and there is often little profit at the beginning. These designers are usually highly motivated and persistent. While they make all the decisions, they also take on all the challenges and disappointments. Handling stress, creatively recovering from mistakes, and knowing when to get help are all critical to this entrepreneur designer's success. The business end of this independent company will take about 90 percent of the designer's time and energy. Structuring the business to take advantage of the designer's strengths and recognizing the tasks where it is more effective in terms of time, energy, and cost to hire a service are key to running a successful business. The business can be set up with the designer as a solo owner or in partnership with another designer. As this type of business grows, some designers look for a business partner to actively share responsibilities or for an investor who is not involved with the operation of the business.

Prior experience in a variety of apparel industry positions can provide a strong base of knowledge and deeper understanding of all that is involved in designing and manufacturing an independent line of clothing. This could include working in retail, working for a large apparel company, working for another independent designer, or doing alterations. Understanding how to balance the costs and rewards of operating an independent company can be challenging. It is common for this designer to hire or contract with sewers to meet the labor-intensive part of the process. Family and friends are often called in to help during busy periods, and student interns can provide valuable help in exchange for learning about the business.

The designer as manufacturer may be oriented toward wholesale clients or directly toward the final consumer. The distinction is important because it will influence how the garments are marketed and merchandised along with the quantity produced, and how the accounting is handled. With a wholesale client, the designer must put together lines that appeal to the potential buyer and merchandise them in a way that makes sense for a retailer. For example, two outstanding jackets may become the centerpieces of the line with supporting tops and bottoms. The shapes

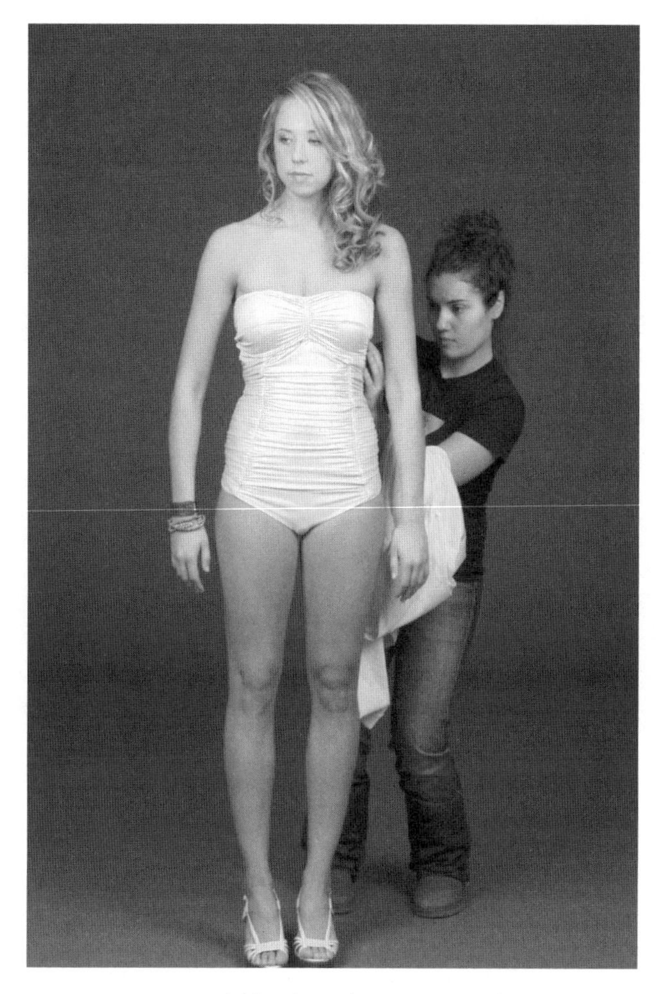

Figure 3.3 Designer preparing model for photo shoot, courtesy of Laura Musekamp, 2009, photographer Ryan Cloutier.

will need to complement different figure types, and the pieces should work together. Orders will determine what is manufactured, and the designer needs to be sure that the original fabrics will be available for production. Billing terms are negotiated at the time of the order, and it is common to offer special incentives, such as quantity discounts or generous payment terms. A permanent wholesale office and rented booth space at trade shows are two options for meeting potential buyers. Sales representatives show lines to potential wholesale buyers and commonly work for several independent designers. Their services are usually based on a sales commission.

Selling directly to the consumer through a retail business, a public or private show, house parties, catalogs, or online creates a different focus for this designer. Preparing

Figure 3.4 Designer's studio, 2007, courtesy of E. Bye.

entries for juried shows, organizing house parties, or developing and maintaining a Web site are examples of the additional responsibilities of this designer. Customers may buy a single item or a complete outfit; thus individual pieces and pairings are more important than a full line concept. Sizing and quantities can be challenging to determine but are critical unless the designer is willing to do special orders. Individual customer service is an important element in working directly with the customer, because repeat customers are core to building this business. Mailing and e-mail lists, advertising in appropriate local media, and open studio tours provide regular contact with the customer.

Custom designer

Excellent customer service skills and a strong desire to work individually with clients are essential for a custom designer. This designer works through the entire design process, consulting with the individual to design a garment that will flatter and fit. The motivation to hire a custom designer usually results from a desire for

Figure 3.5 Craft show booth, courtesy of Karen Bernthal, 2009, photographer E. Bye.

a high-quality garment that is unavailable in the retail market, a need for a special-occasion garment such as a wedding gown, or the need for custom fitting. The ability to support the aesthetic taste of the individual and excellent construction and fitting skills are essential. Some custom designers specialize in a particular garment type, such as tailored suits or dresses, in order to focus their expertise.

Creative problem solving and basic business skills will enhance the success of a custom designer. Self-motivation and the ability to work well on your own are important personal qualities. This designer has great flexibility in choosing a schedule, as well as the type and quantity of work to be contracted. The designer may choose to work independently and keep the business small or may hire an assistant or sewer to enable more individuals to be served. Pricing can be a particular challenge for the custom designer, as many clients will want to compare their work to current ready-to-wear. The value of a custom garment must be realized for the individual to be satisfied. The custom designer is responsible for promoting the business and maintaining a strong reputation. Word of mouth can be the best or worst form of advertising.

FASHION FOCUS FROM THE FIELD: CHAVÉZ CUSTOM CLOTHIERS

Known for his meticulous attention to detail, fit, and quality fabrics, Carlos J. Chavéz is a custom clothier located in Minneapolis, Minnesota, with a second location in Toronto, Ontario. He has U.S. and international clients that come to his studio, or he will travel to meet them for consultations and fittings. He designs custom suiting, shirts, blouses, and evening and bridal wear according to the needs of his individual clients. Equestrian wear is a specialty, and he brings his own experience as a rider to his work.

Clients can expect a very personalized experience focused on luxury and convenience when working with Carlos. During the initial appointment, he discusses lifestyle, needs, and the nature of the event. Individual measurements are taken, and colors, fabric, and styles are selected. The first fitting follows in four to six weeks. All information is carefully recorded and maintained for future orders. He does have a small staff to assist him.

Carlos developed much of his appreciation for fine fabric and tailoring from his Mexican mother, who draped and constructed clothing for her large family in Arizona. Following college, Carlos traveled extensively in Europe, and he continues to travel today, gathering new ideas and inspiration or sourcing fabrics. Carlos gives generously of his time to local design and equestrian groups, including local design students.

Artisan

Driven primarily by aesthetic goals, the artisan designer straddles the worlds of design and art. Garments are created, commissioned, or sold based on their value as artistic pieces. While most pieces remain wearable, their main intent is artistic expression with a focus on content and process. This designer could be categorized as a designer as manufacturer, but the level of production, primarily one-of-a-kind, and relationship to the market are quite different. There was a strong art-to-wear movement during the 1960s to 1980s that brought together the vision, knowledge, and skills of an artist, designer, and craftsman. While textiles continue to be a vibrant medium for artists, wearable art is pursued as a niche market.

Costume designer

A costume designer specializes in garments for the stage, movies, and television. The director provides the designer with the overall vision of a production, and the designer develops sketches with color and fabric selections. Extensive research on the dress of the period in which the script takes place brings authenticity to the production. The movement of the actor, the lighting, the stress of repeated wearing, and the need for quick costume changes require different design solutions than typical streetwear. The constraints of the budget will direct many of the final decisions. Sometimes previously used costumes must be adapted, stock costumes rented, or modifications made to original costume concepts. For modern productions, the designer may act as more of a stylist using purchased garments or vintage store pieces. Costume designers usually start working in a costume shop or doing small productions in their free time. Costume design work is often seasonal, and most designers will need to travel to different production sites in order to work.

Consumer as designer: mass customization

Mass customization is the production of one-of-a-kind products with the economic advantages of mass production. Under this model, products are developed and produced according to an individual customer order. The concept of selling a product before it is made eliminates inventories and dramatically reduces cost. Products are no longer produced with the anticipation of a sale but instead with a sale already secured. The consumer is more likely to get exactly what they want for a price they are willing to pay because they have been involved in the design process. This is not a custom-made garment but one in which individual choice can be realized at a competitive cost.

Getting consumers involved in the design process changes the way clothing is selected and purchased. It also changes the role of the designer. Currently there are three options for a consumer to codesign a product. The first option is to personalize a standard product with printing, embroidery, or applied materials. T-shirts with a personal message or a hat or bag with a business logo are examples of personalization. The second is to offer a garment and allow the consumer to choose from preselected options in style, detail, color, and fabric. The garment type and the sizing are predetermined by the manufacturer. For example, a dress may be offered in one style, a sheath, with a choice of three sleeves (long, cap, sleeveless), two necklines (jewel or scoop), three colors (black, red, purple), and two fabrics (wool, wool/rayon). The customer selects the options, indicates the size, and makes the payment online. The completed dress is delivered several weeks later. The third option is to include personal fit with a standard garment or the previous customized choices. Personal measurements can be taken by the individual and entered online, or measurements can be sent digitally from a file generated from a 3-D body scan. Patterns are then modified and garments produced based on individual customer measurements.

Customized products can be a satisfying option for consumers and offer differentiation from mass-produced products. Consumers' interest in acting as codesigners varies. Some desire having some level of control over the design and fit of their garments, while others have little motivation or time. Apparel designers will continue to play an important role in codesigned mass customization. Their challenge will be to offer design choices that result in garments that are aesthetically pleasing and can be produced at a profit. The consumer must feel that there is an added value to their codesign efforts.

FASHION FOCUS FROM THE FIELD: INDIDENIM

Jeans that are custom fit, with all the styling details chosen personally by the client, are a reality. The mass-customization process at indiDenim is set up to take the consumer through a preselected range of styling options including cut, color, wash, and detailing such as rise, leg shape, and hem and back pocket stitching to make a pair of jeans exactly to an individual's specifications. Guided directions for taking personal measurements are complemented by a series of questions about body shape and fit preferences to make a pair of jeans that is guaranteed to fit. A proprietary algorithm takes all the information and uses it to make a custom-fitted pattern. A customer can also select from predesigned jeans and choose to customize only the fit. Individual measurement files and patterns are stored so that the reordering process is streamlined.

The company is located in Emeryville, California, near San Francisco and offers the option of visiting their studio to have measurements taken with their body scanner. They use an Intellifit scanner with radio wave technology that allows consumers to remain clothed while being scanned. As body-scanning technology becomes more widely available, consumers will be able to have a body scan done anywhere and then send measurements directly to a manufacturer. The jeans are manufactured at indiDenim's plants in Mexico, and the finished jeans are delivered in four to six weeks. The jeans are available for men and women, and the company also offers custom-fitted dress shirts for men.

Figure 3.6 Mass-customization options available from indiDenim, 2009, courtesy of indiDenim.

Supporting the designer

Assistant designer

Designers often start their careers as assistant designers. While their exact responsibilities may vary, their main objective is to help the senior designer achieve his or her goals. It is an opportunity to learn how to fulfill the role of a professional designer, along with the business and design procedures of the company. Much of the day-to-day work will appear routine and might include office work, organization, or running errands. Communication and paperwork with vendors or factories, following up with purchase orders for supplies, or creating design sheets and specification sheets are typical responsibilities. Some assistant designers do sketching, make first patterns, and help evaluate samples. Research and putting together mood, concept, or presentation boards or organizing a fit session may be part of the responsibilities. Sourcing trims and fabric and researching information are important support activities. Assistant designers need to prove that they are organized and reliable and that they can follow directions and complete projects on time. Good product knowledge, the ability to multitask and follow up, and the ability to work in a high-pressure environment are assets. Team players are highly valued, along with confidence that is not overinflated. An assistant designer is successful when the designer and her team are successful.

As the experience of an assistant designer increases, there is usually opportunity for advancement, either within the current company or frequently with another company. The general rule is that if you stop learning it is time to move up or move on. With multiple experiences, a designer's strengths and weaknesses will become clear. Designers will also develop a good understanding of the type of work environments that suit them. A word of caution: the fashion business is small and a strong reputation is extremely valuable. What is said and done at work and in the public eye is critical. Maintaining high-quality work and ethical professional and personal practices contributes to building a successful career.

Two common issues that can present ethical conflicts, particularly for new designers, are factory loyalty and knockoffs. For example, when faced with a decision to move product production from one factory to another based on price, consider that your standing with the original factory will likely deteriorate. Some factories will sever the business relationship altogether. A good working relationship with your factories is extremely important, especially when you need a favor such as a rush order or priority production. However, you may also feel pressure from your own company to keep the costs down, leaving you with a decision to make. Gather the facts and seek the advice of a more experienced colleague. Knocking off another design presents an ethical decision, particularly when a direct knockoff is requested versus using the garment for inspiration. One designer was asked to knock off her colleagues' work from her former company. She knew that they were original designs that had taken considerable time to develop and was very hesitant. Her new employer decided not to proceed with the development, but she had great concern that knocking off the design could potentially hurt her reputation as a designer in a very small field and her ability to get a job in the future.

Technical designer

A technical designer helps transform the ideas and sketches of a garment into a completed sample and is responsible for the garment's construction, size and fit, and quality. A technical package is prepared for the vendor or company manufacturing team and includes a specification sheet with all the critical garment measurements for each size that is requested; a detailed description of the garment with production details such as seam types, finishes, buttons, and trims; a material description; and a detailed technical sketch of the front and back of the garment. This requires extraordinary attention to detail and accuracy. The technical packet is the main communication with the vendor, and the accuracy of the visual elements is critical for those who speak a different language. The technical designer is responsible for all the communication with the vendor or company team. Respecting the expertise of the vendor and any cultural differences is critical to this important relationship.

When samples are returned from the vendor or factory, the technical designer checks the garment against the specifications with a visual evaluation. Critical garment measurements are taken, and evaluation of the fit on a mannequin and a live fit model is conducted. The technical designer organizes and leads the fit sessions, providing background and technical expertise on fitting and construction to help guide the evaluation team. Recording comments and revisions is critical for future communications with the vendor or factory. New technical packages are prepared and the process repeated until final approval is reached.

A strong understanding of construction, production methods, patterns, and fit is essential for a technical designer. Problem solving can be both challenging and rewarding. For example, a pair of shorts was evaluated during a fit session and there was a problem with the short swinging back at the side seam. The general consensus was to have the vendor rebalance the side seam, but on closer inspection, it was determined that the front of the short was cut off grain, causing the swing. This saved the time and expense of remaking the pattern, and it was clear what correction to communicate to the vendor. Another company was fitting a dress shirt that showed diagonal pulls from the shoulder. The shirt had measured within tolerance, but it did not fit. This issue was resolved, and required no further revisions, when the fit model was measured and it was discovered that his cross-shoulder length had increased due to some recent weight lifting.

Textile specialist

With a strong background in textiles and an interest in fashion, a textile specialist provides unique support for a designer. Sourcing fabric and negotiating price and

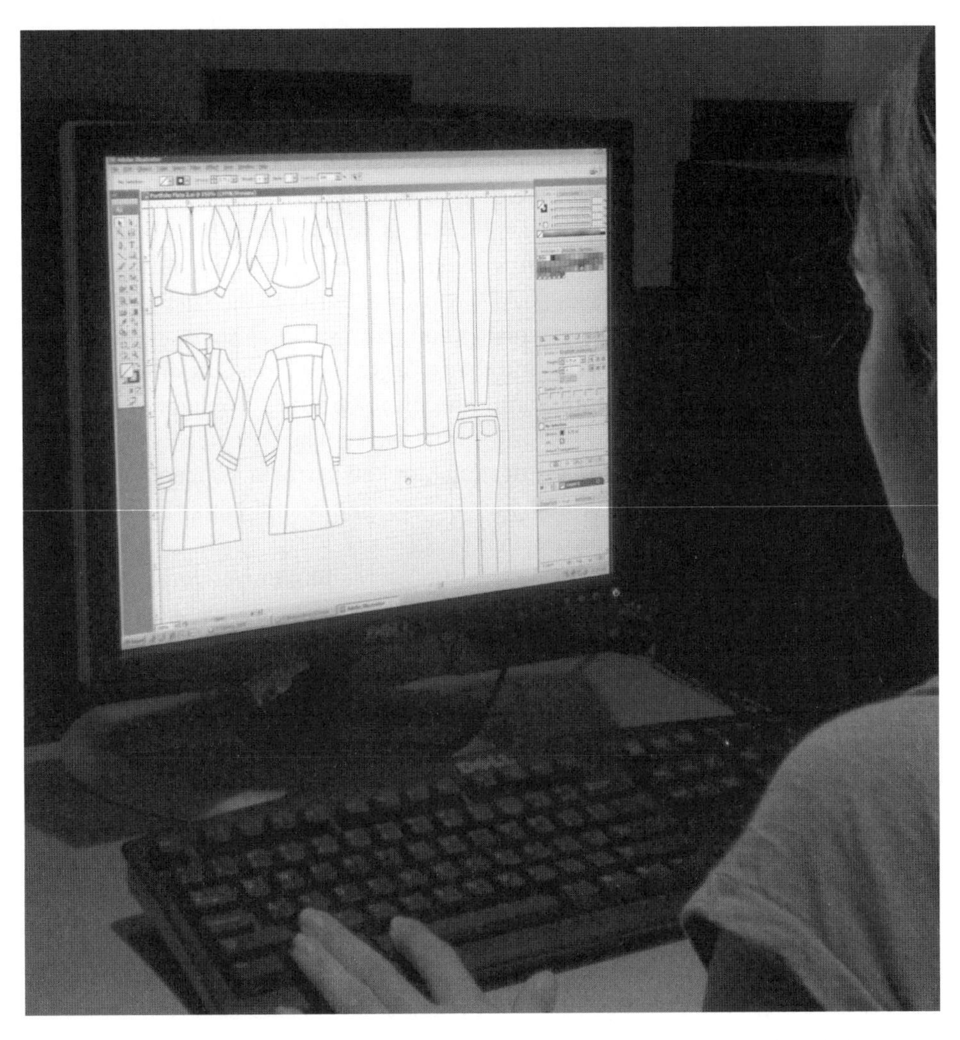

Figure 3.7 Technical designer using Adobe Illustrator to develop technical sketches, 2009, courtesy of E. Bye.

delivery are an important part of the production process. The designer may provide samples, or new samples may need to be found or developed. The textile specialist facilitates this process by working to find quality fabrics on the market or working with textile designers and mills to develop custom fabrics. Textile specialists also research and maintain all the information related to the textiles, including fiber and finish, performance test results, safety testing results, and import and custom regulations. Records are maintained on quality, shrinkage, colorfastness, and returns due to fabric failure. With fabric making up the majority of the cost of a garment, the textile specialist's attention to details contributes greatly to the aesthetics, performance, and cost of a garment.

Textile designer

An in-house textile designer works with the designer to determine the color and concepts for the current season. The background research for this work includes studying designer runway shows, shopping the market, and attending print shows and trend presentations. The colors are then used to develop a cohesive selection of fabrications to be used in the collection. Prints can be purchased from print studios or designed as original art. The design work can be developed by hand or by using a variety of computer-aided design (CAD) software, both off-the-shelf and specialized programs for developing prints, plaids, and stripes. The designs are cleaned to remove extraneous details or marks, and the colors reduced to a cost-effective number to prepare the print for production. The prints are then configured in repeat dimensions and different colorways for manufacturing. The designers collaborate to select the appropriate prints and fabrications for the garment concepts. Preparing packages for print production, keeping an archive, and maintaining the budget are also responsibilities of the textile designer.

This position requires creativity with an understanding of how original textiles contribute to the business needs of the company. Expertise in color, drawing, painting, composition, and math and an understanding of fabric construction are essential for this designer. CAD skills are also important, as is an awareness that being at the computer for long hours can be physically and mentally demanding. As for many design positions, task management, organization, and strong communication skills help support a successful work environment.

Color specialist

A color specialist is responsible for the management processes used to measure and manage the colors for a line. Different fabrics used in a collection must match so that the consumer will be satisfied when buying separate pieces. A color standard is established for each color as a reference for all materials. Colors are measured both visually and with color-measurement technology, and evaluated under different lighting and performance conditions. Evaluation of the results determines whether a sample is accepted or fails. For this specialist, a strong background in color science, good organizational skills, and a good eye for color are valuable.

The color specialist may be responsible for all or part of the process of testing and evaluation. Most often samples are sent out for dyeing and are returned for evaluation, so communication and strong follow-up skills are essential. Due to the great number of variables in the fabric, dye, and the human eye, a tolerance range is used for acceptable matches. However, the color specialist has the responsibility to make the final decision. While it is paramount that the colors match, the work must be completed in a timely manner so that production can continue. Problem solving and negotiation skills are needed to resolve issues with fabrics that won't match: by working with the mill or the dyer or going back to the designer if a new fabric is needed.

With the high demand for color printing by designers using CAD for presentations, the color specialist can also provide support by calibrating the printers to most accurately match the season's line colors. Calibration and maintenance of the color-testing equipment is also the responsibility of the color specialist.

The global designer

It is essential for all designers to have an understanding of the cultures and traditions that contribute to the values of an individual. In the relationships that a designer has with clients, colleagues, business associates, and consumers, cultural literacy is a fundamental skill that impacts behavior. Cultural literacy is the ability to understand and appreciate the customs, values, and beliefs of one's own culture and the cultures of others. Understanding another culture broadens our exposure to practices, ideas, and people that can have a positive effect on our own work and lives. Also, as we begin to understand other cultures, our understanding of our own culture increases as similarities and differences are discovered.

Designers have often looked to different cultures as a source of inspiration but may now be developing garments for consumers from those cultures. A deep understanding of a set of cultural values that are different from or similar to their own may help to prevent stereotyping and bias. Understanding the mores around modesty, use of color, gender roles, or individual or collective orientation can guide design decisions. For example, white is a color of purity in Western cultures, while it is a sign of mourning and death in Eastern cultures.

Communicating with business associates and colleagues around the world, or in the same office, is essential to reaching company goals. Communication may be verbal, written, or visual and face-to-face or electronic, but business success depends on a respectful and productive relationship. This requires understanding traditions for addressing individuals and expected levels of formality. Bilingual and multilingual abilities are of increasing value to designers, whether traveling or working domestically, and their companies. Even knowledge of a few phrases of greeting or thanks in a colleague's language is appreciated as a sign of respect. True cultural literacy takes a great deal of time and effort, because it goes beyond knowledge, awareness, and sensitivity of another culture. Learning to interact effectively with people of different cultures brings a wealth of professional and personal rewards.

Travel as a designer

For many designers travel is a large part of their job responsibilities. Most fashion designers travel several times a year to trade and fashion shows to learn about up-to-the-minute fashion trends. Designers also may travel frequently to meet with fabric and materials suppliers and with manufacturers who produce the final apparel products. Many designers look forward to the opportunity to travel. The experience is exciting: Exposure to new places and people, discovery of new things about the world, personal growth, and the temporary changes are stimulating. However, traveling for business is work, and the expectations for professional behavior are intensified. The job aspects of travel demand that the designer is well prepared for meetings, presentations, or research with all the necessary materials and equipment, along with an alternative plan. Problems will likely arise during travel, but preparation of both business and personal matters can help make the trip successful. Simple elements like having a backup file or the correct converter/adaptor for the computer can become critical issues. Security of data, along with business and personal items, is essential to consider prior to travel. A current passport and any other travel documentation must be arranged in advance. Financial credit or currency that works in your travel destination is critical. Basic information about the destination regarding cultural and business mores, political and economic news, health and safety, climate, and transportation options should be gathered.

Maintaining personal health and energy during travel by eating, sleeping, and exercising well will help keep the focus on the job. Long days with little downtime can make this challenging, so it is important to be flexible and adapt to different situations as they arise. In addition to the planned work, it is important to be prepared to take advantage of experiences that will enhance the design work: museums and cultural events, local restaurants and music, or shopping and people watching. A sketchbook and a camera are essential travel items for a designer.

Work/life balance

In the extremely competitive, rapidly changing, high-stress field of fashion, practices to support work/life balance are vital. Designers need to be physically and mentally prepared to work with dedication and creativity each day. Thus it is important to develop an awareness of what practices and environments support strong work. In addition to good health, creating opportunities for new experiences, planning for play and relaxation, and finding ways to simplify, slow down, and have time for reflective thought are understood to support creativity.

Summary

- The depth and breadth of designer roles depend on the goals of the business and how it is organized. Each role has a unique focus.
- Time, financial, and customer constraints are a constant.
- Vendor designers frequently develop samples in response to a competitive bid request.

- A private-label designer interprets trends to develop exclusive products that meet customers' needs.
- A brand-label designer maintains a consistent brand image, while developing a vision to translate the brand in every garment.
- A freelance designer is an entrepreneur who contracts to complete design work for a client.
- A custom designer is an entrepreneur who designs and constructs garments for individual customers.
- The consumer as the designer makes choices from a predetermined selection of design features in a mass-customization model.
- In addition to a designer, a team of specialized support members collaborate to design and produce apparel products. These include the assistant designer, technical designer, textile specialist, textile designer, and color specialist.
- Cultural literacy is a key skill for a designer that impacts the quality of apparel products and professional relationships.

Vocabulary

- codesign
- cultural literacy
- deliverable
- freelance
- in-house
- personalization
- private label
- sample
- vendor
- wholesale

Discussion

1. What common professional strengths are needed for any design position?
2. What common personal strengths are needed to work independently as a designer? As a member of a team?
3. Compare the primary focus for designers in each role.
4. What are the advantages and disadvantages of working at a larger company versus being a design entrepreneur?
5. What role and connection does each type of designer have to the global marketplace?
6. What opportunities are there for designers to work outside of the traditional apparel industry?

4

HOW APPAREL IS MARKETED

Marketing apparel is central to making connections with consumers. Creating awareness and building the desire for a product are key marketing goals. Because there is often very little that differentiates apparel products in terms of quality and function, the image and reputation of the brand can provide the emotional connection that results in a satisfied consumer and a successful company. The brand image starts with how a company operates, sets priorities, and treats its employees and customers, not with an advertising campaign. Designers have a responsibility to translate the vision and values of the company to consumers in the market through their work (Gobé, 2001). The marketing strategies that a company uses depend on the time, place, consumer profile, available resources, and creative ideas that are generated. Developing relationships that address an individual's aspirations is an approach that can help companies and people achieve their goals. A designer with a large company may have an entire marketing department to collaborate with on projects, while an independent designer needs to rely on his or her own limited resources. Consumers are diverse, but there is an increasing interest in knowing the mission and values of companies that make apparel. Transparency on social responsibility, sustainability, and ethical practices is being demanded: information that goes beyond traditional marketing. This chapter reviews some of the traditional and current marketing approaches that are specific to apparel.

Traditional approaches

Trunk shows

When a designer or a company sales representative makes a personal appearance to show a new line of garments, the event is called a trunk show. Trunk shows take their name from the original practice of transporting collections to the store in large trunks. Today, garments are more commonly transported in garment bags and cardboard boxes. April and May are traditional months for fall collection trunk shows, while September and October are dates to preview spring fashions. Trunk

Figure 4.1 Store window promoting Key to the Cure charity event, 2009, courtesy of Elyse Olson.

shows are intimate events at small boutiques or boutique divisions of a department store, where clients have the opportunity to preview the next season's line before it is available to the general public and talk with the designer. Shows last from one to three days and often include informal modeling, appointments for private consultations, and refreshments. The shows create a perception of exclusivity for the client and offer the opportunity to purchase or special-order garments. Meeting the designer or company representative can have a very positive effect on consumers, who are increasingly interested in who made their clothing and where it was made.

The trunk show can also provide valuable information to the designer. Designers gain insight into the clients' reactions to the line before final production orders are made. A piece may receive a poor reaction and be dropped from the line, or a complementary piece added to fill in a newly perceived gap. Talking with clients in a one-on-one situation is extremely valuable for a designer. The ability to see the garments on the clients and listen to their reactions can provide information about style, fabric, and fit to be used in future line development.

Boutiques usually do not have the space or budget to carry a designer's entire line, so a trunk show is an opportunity for the boutique to present the entire line to its best clients. This creates the opportunity for a sale from garments that would normally not be part of the boutique's wholesale stock. It can also provide a preview of customers' reactions, guiding the owner or buyer on which styles to purchase from the line for the regular season. It is a good way to test a new line to determine whether it is appealing to the boutique's customers. Some boutiques will allow designers and artists to hold special trunk shows to present one-of-a-kind pieces or a complementary line, such as jewelry, as a service to their clients and to bring people into the store. These are usually arranged for a percentage of sales from the trunk show. A trunk show is not a discount sale but a great opportunity for clients to have a very personalized shopping experience that guarantees them access to the season's newest designs.

Apparel showrooms and markets

The wholesale fashion business is conducted with retail buyers purchasing garments from wholesale designers and manufacturers. The majority of this business is conducted in company showrooms or during trade shows. Showrooms are located in a company-owned business location or in a central mart that houses many similar wholesale vendors in the same location. The showrooms are often set up to look like a store and have the business name on the door. Some interior spaces are very luxurious, reinforcing the brand image, while others are more basic with functional rack and display areas. There is usually a desk or table for meeting and often a comfortable place to sit and talk. Many of these showrooms are open year-round, while others are open for business only during market weeks. Major cities usually have established apparel marts with permanent showroom space as well as space to house temporary displays during a market-week event. Special market weeks are held biannually, typically early in the fall and spring. While fashion shows, parties, and promotions are a big part of market weeks, the primary purpose is to buy and sell garments for the upcoming season.

Large trade shows offer another opportunity to take orders and market lines. They are held in rented spaces such as a convention center and are operated by an independent company that specializes in organizing large events and trade shows. This company provides services to the exhibiting designers and manufacturers, the attending buyers, and the media. Some of the leading trade shows include Magic in Las Vegas, Première Vision in Paris, Pure London, India International Garment Fair in New Delhi, and Hong Kong Fashion Week. The shows may have a specific focus, such as ecofriendly fashions or emerging designers. Larger shows are often

Figure 4.2 Invitation to Ruby3 Trunk Show, 2008, courtesy of Anna Lee, photographer Nicholas Marshall.

subdivided by category, for example, men's suits or women's swimwear, to make navigating the show easier for buyers. Buyers and visitors to the trade show must register, prove that they have business at the show, and usually pay a fee to attend. Exhibitors must also register and pay a fee but have the additional expense and responsibility to prepare the booth and promotional materials. Company representatives who will be working must be briefed on the new lines and any changes in business operations such as show specials that offer a discount on an order. These shows often provide the main selling opportunity for a company and generate leads for future business: both critical to a company's success. They are also a chance to do market research, see what competitors are offering, and meet other professionals. Many trade shows have seminars on business- and industry-related topics that can help with professional development or building businesses.

Figure 4.3 Showroom, 2006, courtesy of E. Bye.

Sales representative

A sales representative has the responsibility of selling the line to retail buyers. This sales role is essential to the success of the company, because beyond the financial implications, the sales representative builds important personal relationships with the buyers and represents the values and visions of the company. This person must have a good understanding of the company philosophy, the product, merchandising, and finances. While most represent a single company, some sales representatives work for several smaller, related lines. These are often newer designers or smaller companies with a more regional presence. A sales representative can provide valuable services to a buyer and a new designer. An understanding of how to merchandise the garments and guidance on breadth, depth, and sizing mix can prevent purchasing and production errors.

Sales representatives work from an established showroom, a rented booth during a market show, or a home office. Many sales representatives go on the road making personal visits to local and regional retailers who may not be able to travel due to time or budget constraints. They bring sample garments from the line for the buyers to review, along with a line card and any other information that might be needed to make a sale. The line card has simple sketches or images of all the garments offered with size, color, and price details. Face-to-face meetings are becoming less common with the wide availability of the Internet to share pictures, establish specifications, and negotiate prices and terms. Electronic communication is a strong tool for following up with potential buyers met during a trade show, attracting new accounts, and providing service to current retailers. This is also more convenient for the retail owners because business can be conducted after store hours. Sales representatives usually have all or part of their salary based on a commission earned from selling the line. This commission can be negotiated.

Fashion shows/fashion week

Fashion shows have been the quintessential marketing tool in the fashion industry since Paul Poiret's fashion parades in the early twentieth century. Originally intended to create awareness and desire and promote the designer's work, fashion shows have evolved into a sensory experience and a popular form of entertainment. Attendees come to experience the fashion show: the music, the models, the lights and set design, the special effects, and the gift bags. Each show has a personality and aims to create a mood that reinforces the brand image. The fashion show is not a glamorous event for the designer and the staff but one involving enormous preparation, work, compromise, and stress. Every detail is important and the production of the show requires a large budget of time and resources. The designer's main role at the show, in addition to taking a final bow, is to make sure that everything coming down the runway is being presented exactly as planned.

A fashion week offers a variety of fashion shows that occur continuously over several days in the same location. The event itself attracts fashion professionals, celebrities, and the media, who can conveniently attend multiple shows. Many cities around the world host fashion weeks with a variety of sponsors that range from hair care companies to local governments. Fashion week is usually a time to present new collections and entertain fashion industry supporters. The event is more of a celebration to generate attention and is not focused on selling and buying the line like a trade show. Prominent fashion weeks take place in London, Paris, New York, Milan, Tokyo, and Mexico. The cost of a show during a fashion week can range from $100,000 to $750,000 or more including the venue, music, model fees, hair and makeup, shoes, and invitations (Pasquarelli, 2008). This does not include the cost of the garments in the show. The desired result from this investment is increased visibility that ultimately is measured by future sales.

Attendance at the shows is complementary and by invitation only. The guest list is selected with care and purpose and usually includes editors, CEOs, buyers, and celebrities. While the fashion media report on the garments and trends, the entertainment media report on the celebrity attendees seated in the front row. Many of the most coveted guests cannot attend every show that they are invited to attend, and thus last-minute seating adjustments are often necessary. The prestige of a front-row seat is a hierarchal sign of respect for industry professionals, and it is equally important that it appears full of the most powerful and press-worthy individuals.

A journalist's positive review or a picture in a leading newspaper or magazine is valuable because it attracts attention from both buyers and consumers. Negative press can be disastrous, so cultivating positive relationships with fashion editors is important. Publicity in print, on television, or on the Web increases visibility and strengthens brand identity. Seeing the show live is critical to a fashion professional who is working at the show, reporting and researching the trends and audience reactions. The movement of the garments on the models, the fabrics, and the colors cannot be fully appreciated by viewing an electronic version online (Socha, 2008). The live show makes an emotional impression that is part of the business and pleasure of fashion. Unfortunately, good reviews and publicity do not always result in increased sales (Patner, 2004), an important reminder that the consumer gives the most important critique.

There is evidence of a trend toward smaller, less ostentatious shows. Vera Wang, Betsey Johnson, and Carmen Marc Valvo along with several smaller designers decided not to show in the Bryant Park tents for Fall 2009 partly out of respect for the poor economy. Another motivation is the desire to create a more intimate environment where the clothing can really take center stage. Alternate venues including galleries, event spaces, or store locations are being considered as a way to make the experience fresh. Wang's store became the venue for her line as it was designed to accommodate multimedia presentations and up to 150 guests (Feitelberg, 2008). When evaluating the reward for investment in the big shows, designers may conclude that the big entertainment and media frenzy are not in the best interest of their businesses. With a less intense venue, focus can return to the clothing, allowing a more personal, leisurely interaction with guests (Pasquarelli, 2008). This countertrend for smaller, more intimate shows appears to be the appropriate balance for the grand shows of a fashion week.

Fashions shows also take place on a smaller scale in local venues, put on by retailers, local designers, and community groups. Entertainment and visibility remain the purpose, but these shows seem to put more emphasis on the clothing and the designer. Professional event planners can be hired to coordinate shows. Their experience with the details of presenting a show can be invaluable, as planning a show often requires more work than expected. A retailer may be trying to drive sales by creating desire for its products and services. Putting on a short show at the local mall attracts attention and brings people in to shop. Local designers often hold shows at restaurants or clubs to introduce their work to the community and generate interest and demand. Collaborating with local musicians for an event creates an opportunity to expand the potential audience. Community groups have recognized the entertainment value of fashion shows and use them for fund-raisers and to raise awareness of their group or project. An example is the Chocolate Extravaganza, which presents a chocolate fashion show as part of a fund-raiser for the Make a Wish Foundation. The allure of eating chocolate, listening to music, shopping, and seeing great design, all for a worthy cause, has been a sensory success.

Publications

Historically, printed images were the main form of communicating fashion information. *Mercure Galant* was first published in France in 1672 and is credited with being the first fashion magazine. The French also introduced fashion plates, which provided illustrations of current styles that were mainly directed at local tailors. *Godey's Lady's Book*, first published in 1830, contained many fashion plates as well

Figure 4.4 Chocolate Extravaganza fashion show, design by Laura Musekamp, 2007, courtesy of E. Bye.

as articles and advice for women. Founded in 1892, *Vogue* was sold to Condé Nast in 1909 and has grown to become an international source of fashion and cultural news and commentary. It is published in eighteen countries and written for the Zeitgeist woman of each decade. *Vogue* hired photographers Irving Penn and Richard Avedon in the mid-1940s, and their work encouraged a new, simplified editorial eye. Since the late 1980s, the work of Steven Meisel, Bruce Weber, and Annie Leibovitz has continued to put *Vogue* at the forefront of visual editorials. Currently, publication in *Vogue* is considered a validation for new designs and designers, thus becoming a coveted outlet. Primarily directed toward the nonprofessional, women's fashion magazines have continued in popularity in the twenty-first century and also include *Elle, Harper's Bazaar, Lucire, Cosmopolitan,* and *Glamour,* with many others unique to each country. Today, many of these fashion publications are available online with additional content, and many new online-only fashion Web sites and blogs provide fashion news, images, and commentary.

Validation of a designer and the season's new designs also comes from *Women's Wear Daily (WWD)*, one of the fashion industry's main business publications. Business publications, especially in a daily or weekly format, bring critical information directly to fashion industry professionals, who use it to make decisions daily. A photograph or article in a prominent trade publication reaches this important audience with the power to influence buying, selling, production, and investment. Other trade publications include the *Daily News Record, Drapers, California Apparel News, Sportswear International, Images Business of Fashion,* and *Fashion Biz.* Most of these are available online, and there are numerous online-only trade Web sites directed at fashion industry professionals.

Current approaches

The process of change is fundamental to every facet of the fashion industry, including the changing lifestyle of the consumer. The ways in which fashion communicates and connects with the consumer continue to adapt to new needs, desires, and demands. With consumers who are more educated and confident, fashion and marketing must address their need for authenticity and individuality. Big names and labels hold less appeal, style expectations have been relaxed, and individuals have the resources to make their own decisions regarding fashion (Trebay, 2008). This is evident in popular culture as we select individual songs for our iPod, TiVo our favorite shows to watch at our convenience without commercials, blog with friends we have never met, or create our own entertainment to share on YouTube.

With consumers leading design, it has been difficult for any one designer or brand to provide clear fashion leadership, but perhaps that tradition and the role of designers are changing. For example, consumers can go online and select options for a custom T-shirt, shoes, or a bag, essentially becoming the designer. Some Nike-Town locations have a design consultant who can advise customers on designing a one-of-a-kind product, facilitating the do-it-yourself desire for individuality. Sales associates at Monogram, a luxury line at Banana Republic, are called stylists to reflect their training so that they can help consumers select garments with luxury fabrics and details. The perception of an original, personal brand holds great appeal for consumers who value authenticity and individuality. This is part of a growing fashion democracy that allows each individual to decide what is right for him or her, and this is possible because the market supports a range of styles and price options. Fast fashion, where new styles are available every week, is balanced by the vintage clothing trend; high-end and budget fashion are mixed for style that is affordable for both the wealthy and the budget-conscious; and high-tech garments are met with the countertrend of handcrafted pieces. Retailer Sak's Fifth Avenue took individuality to an extreme when the shoe department received its own New York zip code, 10022-SHOE. The U.S. Postal Service agreed to the distinctive zip code, a model similar to vanity license plates, for promotional purposes. Customers can purchase customized stamps and send mail from the Sak's location.

Celebrity influences

In contrast to this trend toward individualism, there continues to be a fascination with entertainment celebrities from music, film, television, and sports. The public seems insatiable for information about their favorite celebrity, willing to purchase newspapers and magazines with all the details of their lives. Paid celebrity sponsorship of a variety of products helps to build demand for the brand as consumers clamor to have something in common with their favorite star. The fashion industry has used celebrities to directly and indirectly endorse products. Nicole Kidman represents Chanel No. 5 perfume in its advertisements but also subtly endorses Balenciaga when wearing a gown on the red carpet. Many designers donate gowns to the stars to wear at highly publicized events. "Who are you wearing?" is a standard interview query, and the designer's name is included in the photo description.

Celebrity as designer

Fashion is a business that holds great appeal as a way to expand a celebrity brand, and there are many celebrity-named lines on the market. The experience brought from the entertainment industry related to branding and creating new experiences for consumers translates well to the fashion industry. Most celebrities have limited design experience, though some may be involved to varying degrees with developing the concepts for their line, from very hands-on to those who sign a licensing and promotion agreement with little interest in designing the clothing. Most rely on a team of talented but nameless designers to actually execute the design work. There is a large and very interested group of fans who want to dress like their favorite celebrity, making a celebrity apparel line a rewarding business venture. The main focus remains on branding and marketing to the consumer with less emphasis on research and design (Socha, 2007).

The success of the brand and line often depends on the staying power of the celebrity and the quality of the clothing. Madonna collaborated with Margareta van den Bosch, H&M's head of design, to offer a short-term line of garments at H&M. Mary Kate and Ashley Olson have three clothing lines: Ashley controls Row, Mary Kate controls Elizabeth and James, and both work with their line for Wal-Mart. The twins are co–creative directors of a line of shoes with Steve Madden. Beyoncé Knowles started her evening wear line, House of Deréon, with her mother and recently launched a junior sportswear line. Sienna Miller collaborates on the s. miller label with her sister Savannah for their store in London and a small group of retailers in New York. The Rocawear line by Jay-Z was purchased by Iconix Brand Group Inc., and he is responsible for new brand management and licensing. And though most consumers are not aware that the ecofriendly clothes of Edun are designed by Ali Hewson, wife of U2's Bono, the dual appeal of celebrity and green does attract attention.

Designer as celebrity

From a business perspective, most designers need to focus their energy on their primary design responsibilities, leaving little time for celebrity activities. However, designers are well aware of the power of celebrity in creating a brand, and some capitalize on their natural affinity for the spotlight. Poiret may have been the first designer celebrity as he hosted fabulous parties and tours, becoming a showman for his designs. Yves Saint Laurent became a celebrity when he took over the house of Dior at the age of twenty-one. His jet-set lifestyle made headlines and enhanced the designer's mystique. Calvin Klein was part of the New York social fashion elite before his company became famous in the 1970s by moving his labels to the outside of jeans. New York's celebrity circles include Marc Jacobs, who has taken the energy from that lifestyle into his collections, and Tom Ford, who is an international jet-setter with strong Hollywood connections, having once studied acting. Isaac Mizrahi created celebrity status for himself in the movies and as a television talk show host and book author. Stella McCartney was born into a celebrity family, and her name recognition has contributed to her fashion success. However, she places a high value on personal privacy, particularly with a young family, and does not currently appear to be seeking celebrity fame.

Most designers with recognized names have some celebrity status because fashion has such high visibility. They make appearances at fashion shows and charity events and give interviews to promote their business; however, most keep a strong focus on their work and try to keep a private personal life. Donna Karan takes advantage of her designer recognition to lead the Urban Zen initiative, which takes 10 percent of profits from the store to support research and promote patient advocacy, incorporating holistic practice into Western medicine. In contrast, Martin Margiela is a cerebral avant-garde designer known for maintaining an almost reclusive presence in the fashion world, allowing few public appearances, interviews, or photographs. His branding is understated, relying on his product and the subtle trademark label attached with four exposed white stitches, yet his approach and his work are given great attention.

Retail partnerships

Demand for celebrity- and designer-named merchandise has encouraged many retailers to form exclusive partnerships. They have more control over supply, inventory, and markdowns, and the vendor takes on the responsibility of designing and producing the garments. Pierre Cardin is credited as the first designer to license his name in the early 1960s, and the K-Mart company began an endorsement agreement with actress Jaclyn Smith (an original member of *Charlie's Angels*) in 1985 that continues today. Regardless of the business arrangement, retailers benefit from celebrity and designer collaborations because these create an instant brand identity and demand. The concept of massclusivity (short-term, limited-edition lines at budget prices) has translated into increased profits. Celebrities and designers have the opportunity to grow their own brands with an established retailer, provided that they can maintain a meaningful connection with the consumer. For example, musician Lily Allen developed Lily Loves for New Look stores, designer Vera Wang and rock singer Avril Lavigne have exclusive labels with Kohl's, and musician Pete Wentz did an exclusive junior line with Nordstrom. Designers are excited that more people will have access to their clothes and are not concerned that these budget lines will detract from their higher-end lines. In November 2004, H&M sold out their first limited-edition designer collection with Karl Lagerfeld in one day. They followed up with collections from Roberto Cavalli, Madonna, and Rei Kawakubo. Topshop's collaboration with Kate Moss developed into a highly demanded line for the retailer. Target started its collaborations with Michael Graves and Mossimo Giannulli in 1999, launching its GO International concept with Luella Bartley in 2006. Marks & Spencer offered a one-of-a-kind, limited-edition collection from *Sex and the City* designer and stylist Patricia Field.

It has become practical and fashionable to shop at both ends of the retail spectrum. As a result, this trend of designer/celebrity promotion is likely to continue, though some retailers may change direction in order to differentiate themselves. Those in business and marketing will watch closely how the countertrend of individuality alters the direction or power of celebrity influence. With increasing interest in the values and ethics of the people and companies who design, make, and sell clothing, there will be a need for greater visibility and transparency for the business, environmental, social, and philanthropic activities of these celebrities, designers, and retailers. Will the question on the runway continue to be "Who are you wearing?" or will it be replaced by a new question, "How are you giving back and making the world a better place?"

Entertainment factor

There is a strong and growing entertainment factor in fashion. Movies, music, fashion shows, shopping, and parties translate into experiences with the brand and product that create an emotional connection with the consumer. A fashion entertainment experience is able to generate an awareness of a brand that is immediate and engaging, often with the desire to repeat the experience. One of the first fashion television shows was the 1980 groundbreaking *Style* with Elsa Klensch on CNN. Her news show featured live runway video, tours, and interviews with designers from fashion, beauty, and interiors, bringing trade information to the consumer. With a single cameraperson, she talked with designers who were unaccustomed to television interviews and a bit unpolished (Beckett, 2008). Designers in the twenty-first century are more prepared to give an engaging interview for a wide and demanding television and Internet audience. It is now an expected part of their job. Projects that bridge from news into entertainment include documentaries on fashion icon Karl Lagerfeld, Valentino, and *Vogue* editor Anna Wintour, and the five-part BBC series *British Style Genius*.

Movies such as *The Devil Wears Prada*, *Zoolander*, *Unzipped*, and *Garmento* have also spotlighted the fashion industry for a curious public. The success of the *Sex in the City* television series and movie has validated women's obsession with designer clothes and shoes. Some designers gain great visibility when their garments are worn on a show or mentioned in the story line. For example, thanks to Carrie Bradshaw's passion, women everywhere know that Manolo Blahnik designs fabulous shoes. Well-known fashion designers have frequently designed costumes for film and stage, expanding their visibility to a wider audience. Hubert de Givenchy designed costumes for Audrey Hepburn in several of her movies; Hardy Amies costumed films such as *The Grass Is Greener* and *2001: A Space Odyssey*; and Giorgio Armani dressed stars for many movies and television shows. Entertainment creates a broad awareness and demand for fashion information. Watching the annual *Victoria's Secret Fashion Show*, an hour-long advertisement for the brand, has become a home party event for women and men. This interest can also be seen in advertising where there has been an increased use of fictional fashion designers as the central character applying for a bank loan or dealing with a headache.

Reality television has been a popular source of fashion entertainment and information. Makeover and advice shows, such as *What Not to Wear* or *Trinny & Susannah Undress*, are watched eagerly as individuals with little style sense are transformed into attractive, fashionable people. Similarly, *Project Runway* and *Project Catwalk* create great entertainment as aspiring designers compete for a chance to win support for their own line. *Project Runway* semifinalists show their work during fashion week with great press coverage. Despite the drama that surrounds these shows, the public has gained an awareness of the knowledge and skill that are required to design a garment. It has also increased demand for university and technical courses in fashion design.

Figure 4.5 Audrey Hepburn wearing a Givenchy gown in the film *Love in the Afternoon,* 1957.

Shopping has been a clichéd form of entertainment for many women, but new strategies can increase the emotional value of the experience. The Mall of America is a destination shopping site full of entertainment including an amusement park, an aquarium, movie theaters, and restaurants. Many people make the Mall of America a vacation destination because of its entertainment value. Resourceful retailers can create a festive shopping experience by holding private shopping parties complete with wine and discounts, and Women's Night Out is a popular theme to use when several stores and restaurants collaborate on a promotional event. The home party that sells exclusive designs is another trend that is finding renewed energy.

Creating a unique experience in the store through the interior design attracts consumers. The aesthetic environment can draw a consumer into the store and make the visit a sensory experience with music, scent, and dressing rooms that entertain and extend the brand concept. Prada's New York store in SoHo was designed by

Rem Koolhaas and features a wide open space with unusual visual elements, a large round glass elevator, and fun technology including changing-room doors that act like a two-way mirror. Shoppers and tourists visit as part of their travel entertainment to fully experience the Prada brand. Comme des Garçons uses the concept of guerrilla stores located in hard-to-find, makeshift locations to create interest and a sense of immediacy and adventure. The hunt for the store becomes the entertainment, with the location learned through word of mouth. When the focus is on the experience, the clothing may appear to take a secondary role. However, creating an experience or an environment that provides a sense of escape, optimism, or pure enjoyment allows customers to relax and focus on the message and image that are important to the brand.

Museums

The general public's increased interest in fashion has also translated into more fashion-related exhibitions in art, history, and design museums. While many are themed shows that draw from a variety of designers, others are retrospects of individual designers: entertaining and educating the attendees. For example, Superheroes: Fashion and Fantasy at the Metropolitan Museum of Art or Contemporary Japanese Fashion: The Mary Baskett Collection from the Cincinnati Art Museum present popular themes that highlight the work of many known and unknown designers. Retrospective exhibitions including Hussein Chalayan at the Design Museum, Vivienne Westwood at the Victoria and Albert, or Yves Saint Laurent at the De Young Museum, San Francisco, celebrate the work of these designers but also create fashion visibility and perhaps a better appreciation for their work. Though primarily intended to educate the public and honor the designers, the shows can provide a unique marketing opportunity to enhance the brand's relationship with the public. Publicity is provided in exchange for sponsorship of an exhibition, and there is also the opportunity to sell related products in the museum store. Some sponsors may host special events that include parties, opportunities to meet designers, or design competitions. Though Lagerfeld's Mobile Art exhibition was short-lived, the portable building displayed artwork inspired by Chanel's iconic quilted handbag and was intended as a luxury marketing event. The idea combined the appeal of a museum, architecture, fashion, and Chanel luxury. Though it was criticized as lavish and extreme, it likely did little to tarnish the image of Chanel.

The value placed on apparel and accessories by curators from museums worldwide illustrates the importance of fashion to both our historical record and our culture. Many collectors invest in fashion based on either the historic or creative value. A dress worn by Marilyn Monroe was sold at auction for $20,000, and vintage Courreges is sold for thousands of dollars on the vintage market. A consequence of this growing demand is that museums compete with collectors for the pieces. With limited budgets and donors who may prefer to sell their garments, museums are beginning to notice some difficulty with acquisitions. This has implications for the long-term quality and diversity of museum collections.

The growth of the Internet and electronic communication has had a dynamic effect on fashion marketing. While high-fashion designers, retailers, and some consumers are still passionate about hard-copy fashion magazines, the immediacy, speed, and accessibility of the Internet create attractive opportunities and alternatives. Everyone from the wealthy to the budget-minded and the young to the mature is shopping and communicating online. Savvy companies will want to embrace the variety of resources available including Web sites, Twitter, blogs, and social networking sites that are low cost and high impact.

A Web site can be owned by a company, a designer, a publisher, or an independent fashion critic. Dolce and Gabbana, Zandra Rhodes, Josie Natori, and Anna Sui have discovered that their brand can be enhanced on the Web and that their customers do shop online. The North Face maintains a highly interactive Web site that includes online chats with athletes, podcasts from explorers, and training tips. These features make an emotional connection with the company's customers and ultimately drive sales. Marc Jacobs has a Web site with great video and music, images of his collections, news and gossip, biographical information, travel pictures, and information on where to shop. The "Employee of the Moment" video is a fabulous feature that illustrates the value he places on his professional team. Threadless is an online company that uses collective opinion to select its designs. Individuals can submit original designs or vote on their favorite graphic T-shirt design, and then the most popular ones are produced and sold. Most designers and brands maintain highly sophisticated sites that reinforce the brand image as part of a strategy to build a relationship with their customer. The ability to purchase directly from the site varies. Fashion magazines and newspapers also maintain Web sites for easy accessibility and additional content. Some require a subscription and others are open to everyone. Communication formats are changing rapidly to respond to new consumer desires. Suzy Menkes, fashion editor of the *International Herald Tribune* for over twenty years, now blogs with readers online.

FASHION FOCUS FROM THE FIELD: DADADRESS

Jessika Madison-Kennedy launched her business immediately following her graduation from the University of Minnesota. She started online at dadadress.com in the late 1990s at a time when online shopping was very new. Her first Web site of Mod dresses was very basic, but as orders started to come in and the business grew, the Web site became more professional. Madison-Kennedy continued her studies at the London College of Fashion, and that was when the business really took off.

The clothes have a very current, but also timeless, midcentury modern look to them. Dadadress does not follow fashion seasons, and the clientele seems to appreciate the sense of freedom that the line inspires. In her role as designer, Madison-Kennedy must source fabrics, draft patterns, make the samples, and organize production. Finding models, setting up photo shoots, filling orders, and working with sales representatives are also part of the duties. Responsibilities that are unique to the online store include keeping the virtual shop updated and making sure credit card transactions are secure. Dadadress does sell to some boutiques, but having an online showroom keeps her connected to her customer. Dadadress puts a great deal of effort into getting great photos, so customers have a clear idea of what they are ordering. In addition, special attention has been paid to ensuring accurate sizing and good fit. Online shopping has really contributed to making this business a success, with the advantages of low overhead costs and the ability to reach people all over the world.

Figure 4.6 Dadadie Brüke's Web site, www.dadadress.com, 2009, courtesy of Jessika Madison-Kennedy.

Web 2.0 technologies are user generated and have experienced rapid personal and commercial growth. An example is the world of amateur fashion critics, with blogs that include World Fashion News, Fashion Critic, and Fashion Addict. Collectively, bloggers have an enormous influence on their social network whether through an independent blog or an established site such as Facebook, MySpace, or ASmallWorld. On the commercial side, many companies have blogs on their Web sites, and retailers have set up social shopping networks, for example, Stylehive, so individuals can share comments about products from anywhere in the network.

YouTube users create video to make visual connections, and the site is growing in popularity. Fashion shows, both commercial and amateur, are available along with a myriad of commercials, editorials, stories, and personal humor. Companies can create their own channel with programming to market and promote their brand. Retailers, designers, and brands from Neiman Marcus to Alexander McQueen and The Gap have a presence on YouTube. The use of video is expanding to help new designers make connections in the market by selling their work on Shopflick.com. The Shopflick video might show the garment on a live moving model, or the designer may join in to talk about the product. This supports the consumer trend of wanting to know who made the garment and where it was made. The concept is that when consumers have a connection to the designer and brand, they are more likely to purchase the product. While the concept is not new, the method for making the connection is.

Blog or network comments are viral and can have a positive or negative effect on a brand: Items can sell out in minutes or quickly fall from favor. Social networks are often more trusted than established information sources. Word of mouth has always been a traditional form of sharing information with family and friends, but the Internet expands this circle to include people who haven't met in person (Conti, 2008). Due to the uncontrollable nature of social networking, many brands monitor a variety of blogs and may interject an explanation to defend a misperception or extend an invitation for a special event or promotion. Authenticity is a core value of this community, so brands need to identify themselves when communicating. Anyone who poses as a member with exuberant praise for a brand or product is usually discovered. The sites are also a source of trend information for anyone taking an objective view of the activities.

Brand protection

Gucci. Burberry. Ralph Lauren. A brand name immediately brings to mind an image, a feeling, and a lifestyle that distinctively represents a company. Huge amounts of resources are invested to create a brand image that connects to consumers and differentiates the brand in the market. A brand name is valuable and must be protected to insure the integrity and assets associated with it. Protection begins with understanding the legal terms and processes of a copyright, trademark, patent, and license. There are differences in the laws according to the country or state where the business takes place, and a company is responsible for complying.

A copyright protects the use and reproduction of original creative work, which includes images, writings, videos, and sound recordings. It requires the owner's permission to reproduce the work but does not protect the idea. An illustration of a design can be copyrighted, but the design concept is not protected. A copyright can be established by including the © symbol on the object followed by the date and owner's name. A formal registration with a fee is another method of establishing a copyright.

A name or symbol that identifies a product made by a specific company can be established as a trademark. To establish ownership of a trademark, the ™ symbol must be on products or text, the product must be shipped over state lines, and the company must publicly defend the trademark. Once ownership of the trademark has been established, a formal application for a registered trademark ® can be made. Many companies incur enormous legal fees to protect their trademarks. Louis Vuitton's logos, an intertwined "LV" and the Toile Monogram, are trademarked; however, the logos are frequently copied on counterfeit goods, necessitating legal action by the company to protect the integrity of the brand and the consumer. Continued diligence is essential to protect a trademark; for example, Vuitton's first court case was in 1908 to stop the sale of imitation "LV" trunks.

A patent is granted by the government and allows the owner the sole right to make or sell an innovation for a limited period of time. Patents are approved for innovative products and processes that exhibit the practical outcome of original ideas. Few fashion products are designed as a result of technical innovation, thus are not eligible for a patent. However, patented products may be used in a fashion garment including new fibers, finishes, or findings such as Velcro. Filing for a patent is a demanding process that requires the services of a lawyer and a sizable investment and that can take several years for approval.

Licensing is a legal business agreement for a manufacturer to use a brand name or logo on a product. An individual or company can grant a license, for example, Tiger Woods or the Walt Disney Company. A fee, a percentage of sales, or a combination of the two is usually negotiated with minimum and maximum amounts included. Names or logos are licensed to drive sales of the product and must have the visibility and influence to justify the investment. Many consumers assume they are purchasing a designer product, and all that the name implies, when the product carries a brand name. The brand partner may be involved with decisions that impact the brand image such as style, color, quality, and packaging, while some may choose to limit their involvement to signing the agreement. To maintain the integrity of the brand name, it is prudent to carefully monitor the products bearing the licensed name. Consumers will not know the brand partner's level of involvement and associate any quality, performance, or aesthetic evaluation, positive or negative, with the brand. Pierre Cardin was the first haute couture designer to license his name and has shared it with over 900 diverse products from umbrellas to sardines. His license for a line of dishes in 1968 was the first outside of fashion and foreshadowed the practice of lifestyle branding. Unfortunately, the overuse of the Pierre Cardin name has reduced the perception of luxury and quality that was part of the original brand image.

Counterfeits and knockoffs

The fashion industry has a long history of managing the issue of counterfeits and knockoffs. U.S. copyright law, originally based on English common law, does not protect the visual elements of a garment design. In contrast, French law protects the proprietary rights of the author, including the right to authorize the reproduction of the work, affording more design protection. French designers in the early twentieth century depended on licensing agreements to increase their business. The agreement included the use of an approved label to indicate that the garment was licensed. However, they were very concerned about illegal copying, particularly once a design became popular with the public (Troy, 2003). Midcentury, it was common practice for buyers to purchase the rights to individual designs from designers, to be constructed by their own dressmakers. Other buyers were allowed to create knockoff lines that were exact copies of garments they purchased, provided they met the designer's buying minimum (Troy, 2003). These transactions made up a sizable portion of business for many design houses.

Knocking off a design is a frequent practice in the apparel industry as a way to reduce costs and make fashionable garments available at all price points. Manufacturers of lower-cost garments often do not have the budget to develop original designs for their entire line. Other manufacturers want a garment that will generate strong sales. For example, copies of Princess Diana's wedding dress were in shops the next day, selling very well. With the speed of images, some knockoff designs are ready for sale before the originals. This is not an illegal practice but is considered unethical. The practice quietly occurs at all price points; however, most designers will modify the design so that it is not an exact copy, and consider the original an inspiration. This is justified in part on the understanding of common law that no design is considered original. Also, many designers develop similar designs because their research and inspiration have been influenced by a similar environment. Designers must be prepared to support their design decisions and their ethics regarding original work.

Counterfeiting increased dramatically at the end of the twentieth century, in part from the democratization of luxury and the rise of China's economy. The culture of the middle class began to value the status, quality, and image of luxury brands, purchasing products and experiences that were generally not in their budget. Fake versions that appeared to be the real thing became a popular way to create a luxury image without the big price tag (Thomas, 2007). The ethical issues of supporting these illegal activities were almost invisible, but the public became more aware when some products began to show problems with health and safety issues. A knockoff that is presented as the real product is an illegal competitor in the market and may deceive consumers. This has been a common occurrence with online purchases, where the product cannot be closely evaluated until after it arrives (Karimzadeh, 2007). As China increased its manufacturing capabilities and began to participate in the world economy, many new businesses viewed counterfeiting as a profitable venture with little regard for the implications (Thomas, 2007). Large numbers of counterfeit products were easily available for purchase in stores, online, and on the street corner.

Larger companies have the resources to hire lawyers and investigators who can follow leads domestically and internationally, proactively defending their brand. Many organizations, including the World's Customs Organization, are working to reduce the impact of counterfeiting for everyone. The Council of Fashion Designers of America (CFDA) is encouraging the U.S. fashion industry to increase awareness and support new legislation that provides protection for original designs. Currently, the legal system in the United States does not have a way to protect original designs from being copied. The Internet has made fashion images readily available, and purchasing a garment from anywhere in the world is very easy, which increases the

Figure 4.7 Counterfeit handbags, 2005, 2007, courtesy of E. Bye.

opportunity for illegal copying. Creating awareness among distributors, buyers, and consumers regarding who they buy from, how to identify a counterfeit product, and where to report a violation is part of the defense strategy.

FASHION FOCUS FROM THE FIELD: PROTECTION FROM COUNTERFEITS

The consumer is just starting to understand the implications of purchasing counterfeit products. In addition to accounting for approximately 7 percent of world trade, which rightfully belongs to the companies producing the original products, counterfeiters deal in child labor, money laundering, and a range of illegal activities. The purchase of a counterfeit product supports these activities. Customs and border protection have increased efforts to prevent counterfeit goods from entering the United States and have received support from more local city law officials and consumers. In her book, *Deluxe: How Luxury Lost Its Luster* (2007), Dana Thomas highlights the true costs of counterfeit products.

Education and awareness are believed to be the best strategy to reduce demand for fake luxury goods. A reputable place of purchase and a true price are strong indicators of authenticity, whether an item is purchased new or as a vintage product. Authentic luxury products are expensive. Craftsmanship on authentic products is meticulous, and the correct logo and correctly spelled name are displayed on labels, hardware, and packaging materials. The interior is of the same exacting quality as the exterior. Fake logos, poor-quality stitching, or glue may be hard to identify but are critical to an accurate evaluation. It is particularly difficult to assess products online. Everyone is responsible to report counterfeit activity, and this can be done easily and anonymously through a variety of hotlines or Web sites and government offices.

Newer designers or smaller manufacturers may not have the resources to defend their brand and designs. While it is possible that a design may be knocked off, it is unlikely that a less visible designer will be the target of counterfeiting. Counterfeiters want to take advantage of brands that have worldwide recognition—a negative feature of having strong brand awareness. There is clear agreement that counterfeiting a product with a copyright or trademark is illegal; however, some designers are flattered when their designs are copied. It acts as validation that the product was well designed and in demand (Thomas, 2007). Many in the industry believe that imitation is a positive practice because it contributes to the democratization of fashion. In addition, it can be difficult to delineate the distinction between a knock-off and a design that is inspired by another design or honors a master designer. The best resolution will need to offer better protection for original design work while allowing the traditional evolution of trends and style to continue (von Furstenberg, 2007).

Summary

- Trunk shows, fashion shows, and fashion and trade publications are traditional methods of communicating with buyers and consumers.
- Fashion democracy allows each individual to decide what is right for him or her, because the market supports a range of styles and price options.
- The fashion industry uses celebrities to directly and indirectly endorse products and support the brand image.
- While some designers have a natural affinity for the spotlight, most keep a strong focus on their work and try to keep a private personal life.
- Celebrity and designer collaborations with retailers create an instant brand identity and demand, with benefits for each.
- A variety of entertainment formats including movies, television, and books create a broad awareness of and demand for fashion information.
- The interior design of a store contributes to a heightened sensory and entertaining shopping experience.
- The immediacy, speed, and accessibility of electronic communication have had a dynamic effect on fashion marketing.
- Social networks are often more trusted than established information sources, and the comments can have a positive or negative effect on a brand.
- A brand image that connects to consumers and differentiates itself in the market is valuable and must be protected to insure the integrity and assets associated with it.
- Knocking off a design is a frequent but unethical practice in the apparel industry.
- Counterfeiting increased dramatically at the end of the twentieth century, in part from the democratization of luxury and the rise of China's economy.
- Debate continues regarding better protection for original design work while allowing the traditional evolution of trends and style to continue.
- Consumers are directing the future of the apparel industry and providing brands with great opportunities to address their individual needs.

Vocabulary

- authentic
- blog
- brand
- copyright
- counterfeit
- fashion democracy
- knockoff
- license
- trademark
- trunk show
- Web 2.0 technologies

Discussion

1 What role does a designer play in marketing apparel in a large company? As an independent designer?
2 Why are consumers interested in authenticity and individuality?
3 How much influence do celebrities have in the fashion industry? Fashion editors? Bloggers? Justify your position.
4 Are brand-name designer labels worth the price? What does the consumer really get?
5 How will the current environment influence the future of the big fashion show?
6 Prioritize your fashion marketing strategies for a new manufacturer of junior dresses with $5,000 to invest.
7 Argue the pros and cons of design copyright.
8 Find examples of store interiors that offer a unique sensory experience.
9 Is fashion marketing all hype, or is it authentic?
10 What impact does counterfeiting have on the economy?

5

CONTEMPORARY DESIGNERS

Contemporary fashion is international. Designers think, work, produce, and market their garments in both a local and a global context. A British designer may live in the United Kingdom and work for a French company. U.S. designers may live in China and work for an Italian manufacturer. There are fewer boundaries as the diverse background and experiences of a designer contribute to a range of original perspectives in fashion. Though Western fashion has a long history of being the focus of world fashion, there is greater interest in and acceptance of a broader view of fashion. International fashion centers and designers that are growing in visibility and influence are discussed in chapter 6. The following are a sample of influential and visionary contemporary designers. They are designers who excel at their craft, push the boundaries, and have a clearly defined philosophy. The designers are selective when sharing information about their personal lives. These contemporary designers are fully engaged with the needs and desires of the ready-to-wear and prêt-à-porter markets and understand that commitment to social and environmental responsibility is valued. The generous and ethical character of many of our contemporary designers is a fabulous model that reflects positively on the apparel industry.

Designers develop many different talents and take their work in a variety of directions. The Innovators reach out to new possibilities inspired by both old traditions and new technology. The Editorial Voices courageously use their work to bring critical and thought provoking ideas into the public arena. The Altruists have embraced the larger world with thoughtful practices, and the Emerging are just laying the foundation for what is to come as they develop into mature, responsible designers.

The innovators

Issey Miyake (1938–)

Issey Miyake is a brilliant designer. His approach to making clothing is built on the balance between tradition and innovation. He has deep respect for the ancient handcrafts of Japan and other cultures, using them as an anchor to explore and develop new methods of making clothing. He established the Miyake Design Studio in 1970 as a place to collaborate and help ideas take shape with a diverse team of talented individuals.

Miyake showed his first collection of knits in Paris in 1973. He was part of a changing force in fashion exploding from Japan that included Kenzo Takada, Yohji Yamamoto, and Rei Kawakubo. Their divergence from Western fashion held references to artistic collaborations that were more sculptural in form. Miyake has been fascinated with the space between the body and the garment, and collaboration with William Forsythe for a dance production in 1991 led to the development of his well-known Pleats Please line. Miyake has designed many of his garments to enhance the organic movement of the body. His original process, based on the traditional practice of Shibori, produces a light, textured fabric that resembles tiny

Figure 5.1 Black Pleats Please evening dress by Issey Miyake, polyester, 2001, courtesy of the Goldstein Museum of Design.

pleats. The garments travel well because they do not wrinkle and can be washed and dried overnight. In collaboration with Dai Fujiwara and a team of young designers, Miyake developed A-POC (A Piece of Cloth). A-POC is made by using computer technology to knit or weave clothing that begins with a single piece of thread and can be cut into customized designs by the consumer. Miyake continues to put his energy into research as his main interest is in the future. This is also exemplified through his nurturing of talented young designers.

Miyake established the Issey Miyake Foundation in 2004 to explore how all mediums of design affect our daily lives. The foundation helped to establish the 21_21 Design Site in Tokyo as a research center for design. It is a place to encourage thinking about design and a place for making the objects of design. His work has been honored and exhibited internationally in multiple venues. Miyake's spirit and curiosity are unsurpassed.

Miuccia Prada (1949–)

With a PhD in political science, Miuccia Prada seemed unlikely to take on the design responsibilities at her family's luxury leather goods company in Milan. Fortunately, she has the courage to take risks and keen observation skills that she has been able to translate into apparel. Her strength is in her ability to successfully combine unusual materials with an original purpose. In 1985, a line of black, unlabeled, durable, and finely woven nylon handbags was her first success with this concept. Her use of nylon to create a sleek, high-end handbag was innovative and resulted in making the Prada label a must-have for the fashion elite.

Prada's first collection in 1989 received critical acclaim for the pure, austere lines of her designs. She focuses on understated luxury that appeals to a more private individual. Inspired by her own wardrobe of clothing with a natural bohemian style, she started the Miu Miu bridge line with an aesthetic that is less austere and a bit more daring. With the help of her husband and business partner, Patrizio Bertelli, the company expanded its portfolio of brands in the pursuit of becoming an international conglomerate. Prada presents a philosophy of understated luxury using precise craftsmanship in her original, graceful, and minimalistic designs. In recognition of her work, she was given the International Award of the Council of Fashion Designers of America (CFDA) in 1993. Prada and her husband are passionate supporters of contemporary art. They established the Prada Foundation with the space and a staff to facilitate the exhibition and publications of new contemporary artists. Prada's view of the world is reflected in her designs, and her work is a distinctive addition to fashion.

Nicolas Ghesquière (1971–)

Even as one of *Time* magazine's 100 most influential people in 2006, Nicolas Ghesquière is not interested in fame. As head designer at Balenciaga, he is much like the master in his desire for privacy, with no interest in marketing his personal persona. With great respect for Cristóbal Balenciaga's elegance and inventiveness, Ghesquière has reinvented the staid house with a combination of street style and history, making him both influential and in high demand. Ghesquière has the sensitivity to look beyond the styles and trends of the past or present and connect to the mood, values, and life of the women he dresses.

Ghesquière's talent for draping clothing around the body developed from a series of apprenticeships starting with Agnès B in Paris when he was fifteen. Three years later, he was working with Jean Paul Gaultier. At twenty-one, he began to freelance and designed an anonymous line of knitwear. Ghesquière joined Balenciaga in 1995 and became head designer two years later. After gaining some experience, his 2001 collection put him in the forefront of fashion. His architectural garments are rich in meaning and executed to perfection. His women's trousers have an almost cult following due to their flattering cut. The Gucci group now backs Balenciaga, with a focus on luxury ready-to-wear and all the supporting businesses. The expansion of the company with a new Balenciaga store in Los Angeles, California, combines a focus on the future and sustainability.

Ghesquière is dedicated to the success of the house. His fusion of high-tech and classic fabrics and his interpretation of the 1980s melded with the patrimony of Balenciaga have made him a true original. One inspired silhouette created with skinny pants and a blouson top became a principal look in the early twenty-first century. Garments that appear simple in form and beautifully encircle the body are possible due to his technical expertise in tailoring and draping. Considered a scientist of clothing, he was honored by the French government in 2008 with the Chevalier of the Order of Arts and Letters. With Ghesquière, the best is yet to come as he indicates that he has saved his own name for a future label that will be very new and different.

Marc Jacobs (1963–)

Marc Jacobs is synonymous with youth, vitality, and energy. As creative director of Louis Vuitton since 1997, he has a talent for keeping his vision modern and contemporary for both the LV line and his own labels: Marc Jacobs and Marc by Marc Jacobs. He studied at the Parsons School of Art and Design and won the prestigious Perry Ellis Golden Thimble award. His senior show was so impressive that Robert Duffy contacted him the next day and asked him to work on a project for Ruben Thomas Inc. That connection developed into a partnership that continues today. The team was hired by Perry Ellis in 1989; there, Jacobs designed his radical grunge collection. It received kudos from fashion critics and customers and prompted the Women's Designer of the Year award from the CFDA in 1992. He has gone on to win seven CFDA awards.

Jacobs and Duffy opened the first Marc Jacobs store in the Soho district of New York City in 1997, and they have since expanded to over 100 stores across the world.

Jacobs and Duffy have made it a high priority to give back to all the communities in which they have stores, resulting in support of over sixty charities. Each year, Jacobs promotes one worthy cause, with recent examples including the Human Rights Campaign, New York University Interdisciplinary Melanoma Cooperative Group, and Breast Cancer Awareness.

Jacobs and his clothing are hip, and he understands what his customer wants to wear. He has the confidence to make a statement that does not follow the trends. His approach to fashion often references the past but with a less serious and more wearable interpretation. Jacobs's use of color and texture are strong elements of his designs. His collaborations with Steven Sprouse, Julie Verhoeven, Takashi Murakami, and Richard Prince have resulted in innovative bags that showcase their artwork for the LV line and have been very successful. Collaboration is a core value for Jacobs, who proudly credits his full team for the garments and bags that are designed, with him as a member, not the director: a truly innovative perspective.

Linda Loudermilk

Linda Loudermilk's vision is one of sustainable fashion that is glorious, attractive, exciting, and a little radical. She refers to this concept as luxury eco. This Los Angles–based designer was showing in the Paris couture shows in 2002 when she realized that her work needed to have more depth and meaning. She began to work with fiber and textile companies to source and develop original sustainable fabrics that were produced without pesticides or toxic processes. These include organic cotton, reclaimed antique lace, recycled bottles, and *sasawashi*, a blend of Japanese paper and *kumazasa*, an herb. Her leadership in the development of luxury sustainable fabrics introduced a timely and smart concept to fashion. Her work counters the perception that all things sustainable are utilitarian and unattractive.

Loudermilk looks to nature as inspiration to guide her design work. Her pieces are sculptural, well cut, chic, and modern. Trained in costume design at Oxford University and by her grandmother, who was a couturier tailor, she has chosen to have her pieces hand finished and made primarily in the United States. The focal point of her garments is the fabric, which she highlights using clean silhouettes and unusual details. According to *Elle* magazine she is the "Vivienne Westwood of eco."

In addition to her innovative work, she has developed the Eco-Luxury Stamp of Approval, the only one of its kind. Companies can apply to use the stamp as a sign to consumers that the products or services carrying the stamp are ecofriendly and superior in luxury, quality, design, and craftsmanship. Loudermilk was named one of the top twenty innovators to watch by *W* magazine. She supports the Children's Health and Environmental Coalition, which is particularly interested in the connection between environmental toxins and cancer.

Figure 5.2 Linda Loudermilk Spring Collection 2008, photographer Stephanie Diani, courtesy of Linda Loudermilk.

Editorial voices

Katharine Hamnett (1947–)

Katharine Hamnett has her roots in international fashion and is credited with establishing popular trends in power dressing, distressed denim, garment dyeing, and retro fashion. Her slogan T-shirts have promoted numerous social and political causes over her long career, including "Choose Life," "Say No to the Euro," and "Use a Condom." After graduating from Central Saint Martins in 1969, she immediately launched an extremely successful business that showed on the catwalks in every major fashion center. She received many awards for her work including the 1984 Designer of the Year award from the British Fashion Council, but by 1989 she was bored with her success. Hamnett began to explore the impact of the clothing industry on the world's environmental and human resources and decided to move her business in a new direction.

After considerable, but unsuccessful, efforts to change the industry from within, Hamnett redirected her energy toward raising consumer awareness about critical environmental and worker issues in the apparel industry. She visited Mali cotton farmers with Oxfam, an organization dedicated to ending poverty and injustice worldwide, in 2003 and returned with a commitment to promoting organic cotton. She believed that organic practices would address issues of poverty for the farmers and have less impact on the environment. Hamnett proceeded to cancel her many licensing contracts because they would not agree to produce her products ethically. In 2005 she revived her Hamnett menswear and women's wear lines and included

Figure 5.3 Love T-shirt, 1988 reissue, by Katharine Hamnett, 2007.

her original 1980s fashion slogan T-shirts, now made with organic cotton to the highest ethical and environmental standards in the world. She believes that people are starting to understand that how we consume will determine the future of our world. She continues to speak out about controversial world issues and is currently a professor at the University of the Arts London.

Alexander McQueen (1970–2010)

The radical vibrancy and emotion of Alexander McQueen's designs were based on solid technical training that he began as an apprentice with bespoke tailors on Savile Row. He also worked for theatrical costumiers Angels and Bermans, and Koji Tatsuno, known for their tailoring and craft techniques. A period of work for Romeo Gigli exposed him to Italian manufacturing before he returned to London in search of a tutor position at Central Saint Martins College of Art and Design. Instead, he enrolled as a student and received his master's degree in fashion design in 1991.

McQueen's work was known for its technical excellence and themes that explored juxtapositions between contrasting elements such as frailty and strength, tradition and modernity, and soft and hard. These included a reflection on the environment through Charles Darwin and modern industrialization, comments regarding the collapsed economy that has no future vision, and a tribute to friend and supporter Isabella Blow. His own label made instant headlines with a shocking collection, Highland Rape, which included his infamous low-cut "bumster" pants. He was hired as chief designer at Givenchy in 1996, though it was a poor match, as McQueen considered the founder irrelevant. He left in 2000. McQueen began a new partnership with the Gucci Group in which he negotiated ownership of 51 percent of his label and gained the title of creative director and creative freedom. The company's growth was strong and included collaboration with Puma to create a special line of sneakers, as well as with Samsonite luggage and MAC cosmetics. McQueen shared his talents with charity fund-raising projects that included the Pinkridges scarf for Breast Cancer Care, Bags for Life to support the United Nations Refugee Agency, and the Black Art fashion show benefiting the London-based HIV charity Lighthouse.

McQueen's shows were theatrical presentations and were intended to shock with illusion, controversy, and seemingly little regard for the commercial value of his work. His goal was to draw attention to his work and his message. His awards include Best British Designer of the Year (four times) and International Designer of the Year from the CFDA in 2003. He was recognized as a contemporary leader in fashion with a vision and commitment that made him an icon of the fashion world. He was a romantic at heart, exploring both the light and the dark of the world, with the commitment to embrace his imagination.

Dries Van Noten (1958–)

Born into a family of tailors, Dries Van Noten has an unconventional perspective on fashion. He designs individual items rather than developing a collection around a single silhouette or theme. This has proven successful for him, as evidenced in a strong international business of menswear, women's wear, and accessories. Van Noten is comfortable sitting to the side of mainstream fashion and is unconcerned with reviews from the fashion press. He questions the purpose of haute couture, wondering why someone would design a garment for show that cannot be worn in real life. His integrity and commitment to beautiful, wearable clothing are the focus of his practice.

Van Noten lives and works in Antwerp, Belgium, and was instrumental in creating the visibility that made Antwerp a fashion city. This was accomplished with a group of designers called the "Antwerp Six" who met at the Antwerp Royal Academy in the early 1980s. Along with Van Noten, Dirk Bikkembergs, Dirk Van Saene, Ann Demeulemeester, Walter Van Beirendonck, and Marina Yee (who replaced original member Martin Margiela) created fashion shows and events that caught the attention of the international fashion press. The presentation of their inventive styles and excellent craftsmanship received unprecedented praise during the 1988 London Fashion Week.

Van Noten is known for incorporating folkloric elements including embroidery and beading in his internationally inspired designs. His juxtaposition of prints and strong use of color are highlighted in very wearable shapes. He has also made an effort to create sustainable spaces for his business, starting with his first store, which was in a historic 1831 building in Antwerp. In 1989, he restored a historical department store that had once housed his grandfather's greatest competitor, making it home to his store Het Modepaleis. His Paris boutique opened in 2007 in a seventeenth-century building that Van Noten worked to preserve. He has a strong but unassuming voice in the fashion world and was recognized with the International Award of the CFDA in 2008.

Vivienne Westwood (1941–)

Eccentric. Provocative. Wonderful. Vivienne Westwood has been designing clothing since 1971 with all the bravado her customers expect. With her partner, Malcolm McLaren, she opened a shop called The End and launched punk fashion using rubber, safety pins, and offensive T-shirts. Her reputation was assured when the punk band the Sex Pistols, managed by McLaren, performed in her designs. By 1981, punk fashion had begun to subside, and Westwood presented her first collection, Pirates. The colorful and romantic collection was based on eighteenth-century men's clothing and featured full, flowing shirts and exaggerated pants. A Paris show in 1983 brought her global recognition as an avant-garde designer, and the end of her collaboration with McLaren. Westwood showcases British wools, tweeds, tartans, and linens in her collections, to the delight of her country, and was named British Designer of the Year in 1990 and 1991. Westwood often works historical and political references into her work in a parody of establishment styles, with collections including Savage, Nostalgia of Mud, and Buffalo Girl.

Despite her nonconformity, she has been a professor of fashion at the Vienna Academy of Applied Arts and the Berliner Hochschule der Künste. She was made Dame in 2006 by the Prince of Wales, marking the occasion by repeating her infamous practice of not wearing her knickers. Westwood lives a modest life with few possessions and prefers cycling to work. Her charitable work supports organizations from the National Society for the Prevention of Cruelty to Children to the human rights group Liberty. Independent with a curiosity about how things work, this forward-thinking designer continues to design witty, revolutionary, and glamorous collections.

The altruists

Betsey Johnson (1942–)

Betsey Johnson's first design position was with Paraphernalia, a clothing boutique that employed popular young London designers, including Mary Quant and Paco Rabanne. She brought her own energy to the 1960s youth movement and has continued to create high-spirited, whimsical, and colorful clothing throughout her career. In 1999, the CFDA honored her with the Timeless Talent award, which was created to recognize her influence on fashion.

Early in her career, Johnson's ties to pop culture were strong. She dressed John Cale of the Velvet Underground and designed for Alley Cat, a trendsetting label for 1970s rock clothing, with bohemian and ethnic styles. She started her Betsey Johnson label in 1978 in partnership with Chantal Bacon. Their original store in Soho has grown into over fifty stores worldwide and a strong licensing business representing the Betsey Johnson lifestyle. Her most recent project has been the creation of the Betseyville hotel in Mexico.

Johnson is a breast cancer survivor and huge supporter of the fight against breast cancer. She brings her trademark energy to her public appearances and fundraising efforts, including as honorary chairperson for the 2003 Fashion Targets Breast Cancer. She also collaborated with Geralyn Lucas, the author of *Why I Wore Lipstick . . . to My Mastectomy*, by designing a complementary T-shirt to mark the launch of Courage Nights in her stores.

From her first recognition as winner of *Mademoiselle* magazine's guest editor contest in 1964, Johnson has gone on to be the youngest winner of the Coty award, is honored on the Seventh Avenue Fashion Walk of Fame, has numerous lifetime achievement awards, and was named Designer of the Year in 2006 by the American Apparel and Footwear Association's Image Awards. Johnson continues to be a fashion leader, confidently listening to her own voice and enjoying work and life with a contagious enthusiasm.

Donna Karan (1948–)

Donna Karan is a leader. Her first line introduced a system of dressing that was professional, easy-to-wear, and luxurious. With her cashmere and spandex bodysuit as the core piece of her design concept, she gave women a sense of security and freedom of movement. Luxurious knit skirts, jackets, and pants were designed to be worn over the bodysuit. A feeling of sensuality is evident in her clothing, but above all, they flatter and function for the women who are wearing them.

Figure 5.4 Navy blue bodysuit, jacket, and skirt by Donna Karan, wool jersey, 1970–1979, courtesy of the Goldstein Museum of Design, gift of Andrea Hricko Hjelm.

Her professional career began at Anne Klein after she had studied for two years at Parsons School of Design. She became head designer after Klein died in 1974 and was joined by Louis Dell'Olio the following year. Karan is credited as one of the innovators of the bridge line and lifestyle dressing when she introduced Anne Klein II. Karan founded Donna Karan New York in 1984 with her husband, Steven Weiss, and introduced the DKNY line four years later. Expanding the company with menswear, jeans, accessories, hosiery, fragrances, and cosmetics, she sold the company to LVMH Moët Hennessy - Louis Vuitton in 2001 and now serves as chairwoman and chief designer. Karan has been recognized by the CFDA six times for her excellence.

Karan's interest in Eastern philosophy and meditation has been a foundation for her approach to living. With heart, body, and soul, she balances her artist's need for beauty and her woman's need to nurture. The founding of the Urban Zen Foundation with its focus on advancing well-being, advocating for children, and preserving cultures follows a long record of philanthropic work supporting women, children, AIDS and cancer research, and the arts. Karan also gives back by spending time with students at Parsons. Karan focuses on lifestyle as the core of her designs, and her strength will continue to inspire the people who feel her touch.

Stella McCartney (1971–)

Stella McCartney has built a reputation for herself as an earth-friendly designer. She has consciously built her company with core values that center on environmentally friendly choices, from fabrics and manufacturing to wind-powered energy sources. McCartney began her career as an apprentice for Christian Lacroix and with tailors on Savile Row. She graduated from Central Saint Martins College of Art and Design in 1995 and began her own label that same year. She proved her talent with the success of her first collection for Chloe in 1997, which included an updated pantsuit and delicate lace camisoles and petticoats with fine tailoring. Her sense of the romantic and skill in tailoring have resulted in a wonderful mix that has become her signature.

In a joint venture with Gucci, McCartney presented her first collection in 2001, building a business that includes perfume, an organic skin care line, and collaborations with artists including Gary Hume, David Remfry, Robert Crumb, and Jeff Koons, using his prints on dresses and accessories. A long-term partnership with Adidas began in 2004, and this is seen as a lifestyle brand that complements McCartney's vision for her company. Making fashion available for the masses, she designed a line of apparel for H&M that sold out in one day. She has also collaborated with Bendon lingerie and LeSportsac.

McCartney does not use fur or leather, in support of her values as a vegetarian and in honor of her mother's work for animal rights. Even with her famous parents, Sir Paul and Linda, she has proven herself an independent, talented, responsible, and ethical designer. Her leadership as an earth-friendly designer places her at the forefront of fashion that is both ethical and profitable.

Yohji Yamamoto (1943–)

In a simple palette of black, navy, and white, elegantly constructed shapes inspired by menswear and sophisticated layering are the core of Yohji Yamamoto's garments. With silhouettes that range from oversized to fitted, his wit and respect for his clients make him a favorite of his peers. A graduate of the Keio University and Bunka Fashion College, he presented his first collection in Tokyo, under his label Y's. Yamamoto's reputation and success grew after he began to show in Paris, developing a higher-end Yohji Yamamoto collection and a home line.

Yamamoto has found a balance between his commercial business and his more artistic interests. As a way to expand the brand, he has developed fragrances with Procter & Gamble and established a partnership with Adidas that resulted in the creation of the Y-3 label in 2003. Yamamoto is very active in the international arts community, collaborating on film projects, opera costumes, and ballet sets. The Yohji Yamamoto Fund for Peace was established to advance the development of China's fashion industry, a gesture of reconciliation for a long-standing conflict between Japan and China. Funding for a two-year scholarship for an emerging Chinese designer is one example of support. Yamamoto has been called a philosopher, artist, and poet, and his work has been exhibited in museums in Tokyo, Florence, Paris, and Antwerp.

Yamamoto's pieces have become timeless, because they are practical and very wearable, rising above the trends of fashion. He has great respect for our world's resources and economic health as well as a delight in and enjoyment of life. Added shots of bright color and his use of allusions in his designs balance the intellectual and abstract tone of his clothing. Yamamoto is masterful in his use of texture, light, and shadow. His clothing has a flow and a grace that feels sensual and spiritual. Yamamoto continues to challenge Western aesthetics with open, innovative concepts for dressing.

The emerging

Derek Lam (1967–)

Derek Lam has an inherent ability to create feminine, wearable clothing cut with attention to timeless details. The influence of Asian respect and discipline in his clothes is evident. With his use of clean lines and modern, luxurious fabrics, Lam reinterprets American sportswear with elegance and attention to the qualities of beautiful handwork. Lam launched his own label in 2003 with business partner Jan-Hendrik Schlottmann, winning the CFDA Perry Ellis-Swarovski Award for Emerging Talent in Womenswear in 2005. In 2007, he won Accessory Designer of the Year at the 2007 CFDA Awards. His success comes after twelve years of experience working with Michael Kors following his graduation from Parsons School of Design.

Lam is inspired by Egon Schiele, a figurative painter known for his intensity and expressiveness, and the worlds of art and architecture. He pays close attention to how women live in modern society, incorporating both wearability and luxury into his garments using pretty, feminine fabrics and crisp silhouettes. He is known globally through his work, which has been exhibited at the Kennedy Center's The New China Chic exhibition in 2006, and at Victoria and Albert Museum's exhibit of significant New York fashion. Lam has been creative director for Tod's since 2006. His eye for detail, love of classic lines, and understated luxury complement the brand.

Thakoon Panichgul (1976–)

With a business degree from Boston University and experience as a merchandiser and journalist for *Harper's Bazaar,* Thakoon Panichgul brings a selective eye to his Thakoon line, launched in 2004. Inspired by the process of making clothing and careful attention to finishing details, he creates garments that are modern and polished. Panichgul designs for a confident woman, considering what she wears and what she wants. His timelessly feminine designs are delicate but wearable, with a playful spirit. He moves from the ethereal to the urban with great flexibility, in part from his training at Parsons School of Design. Born in Thailand and growing up in Nebraska, he has great respect for the past but his vision is modern.

Panichgul has been recognized with three nominations for the CFDA Swarovski Award for Womenswear. In addition to his own line, Panichgul designed for the luxury retailer Hogan, NineWest, The Gap, and the United Kingdom's fair trade fashion favorite, People Tree. His signature style is still evolving, but he has been consistently successful with his print dresses, often executed with a surrealist touch. He is also adept at contrasts, for example, lace and tulle on a trench coat. His increasing visibility and retail successes continue to propel the Thakoon line forward.

Christopher Kane (1982–)

Christopher Kane has edged toward the forefront of fashion with a fresh aesthetic that bursts with sophisticated energy. After his training at Central Saint Martins, he started his own label in partnership with his sister Tammy, a textile designer, who also handles the financial end of the business. These Scottish siblings experiment with color, fabrics, tailoring, and embellishment to offer a new definition of feminine. A recipient of the British Fashion New Designer of the Year Award in 2007, only a year after his graduation, Kane is on an upward trajectory. He showed his master's degree graduation collection in Harrods after receiving their Design Award and has collaborated with Donatella Versace on several projects. His collections have all received strong reviews by the fashion elite and by women, who continue to buy out his pieces. As Kane and his sister work to evolve their vision into a brand, it will be worth watching this new force in fashion.

Laura and Kate Mulleavy

These sisters, graduates of the University of California, Berkeley, taught themselves the technical side of design by taking apart other designers' dresses. They began experimenting in a workspace behind their mother's home in Pasadena, California, creating stories of fantasy to inspire their work. Their label, Rodarte, is known for its soft, feminine, and almost ephemeral gowns. They have adopted a practice of using intricate hand-stitching and traditional techniques. The sisters are talented and meticulous with a strong eye for detail that is in part due to Laura's background in English literature and Kate's knowledge of art history. Since their spring 2005 debut during New York Fashion Week, their work has been a highlight for the fashion press, buyers, and those who walk the red carpet. Their intricate art is part of the permanent collections of the Metropolitan Museum of Art and the Fashion Institute of Technology Museum.

Figure 5.5 Dress by Rodarte, shown by designers Laura and Kate Mulleavy at the Swiss Textiles Awards on November 13, 2008, courtesy of Swiss Textile Federation, photographer Sonja Hugentobler, Trendspot, model Tamara P@Profile, London.

The Mulleavy sisters are beginning to expand their line to include more wearable day pieces, and they had a successful collaboration with The Gap. They were awarded the 2008 CFDA Swarovski Emerging Womenswear Designer award, and the 2008 Swiss Textiles Award, which supports international expansion for new designers. Without formal training in design, Laura and Kate took a risk that has brought a new, emotional expression to their garments. Their respect for the craft has allowed them to create a strong foundation to support the future potential of Rodarte.

Designers behind the brands

The designers who work under their own names are generally well known. They have achieved success with hard work, the experience of apprenticing for a known designer, and some measure of financial backing. They have a clientele who supports their work and have achieved global visibility. Named designers have developed a brand that carries their name or promotes them as the creative designer or director of the brand. However, many talented designers are the creative force behind a brand that does not carry their name. Some in the fashion industry may recognize their name and their work, but most consumers have no idea who they are. These often invisible designers are responsible for the success of the brand and deserve recognition for their excellence.

Burberry: Christopher Bailey (1971–)

Named one of the world's most influential designers by *Forbes* magazine in 2005, Christopher Bailey has been an invaluable addition to Burberry since his start in 2001. Combining classic Burberry style with London street fashion, he has reenergized the outerwear company, which was first established in 1856. His creative direction under the Prorsum label has moved the house to the center of the fashion world.

Bailey was trained at the Royal College of Art in London and invited to work for Donna Karan in 1990 following her visit to the college. A meeting with Tom Ford in 1993 moved him from New York to Italy as a senior designer at Gucci. His ability to respect the Burberry traditions in combination with his use of modern silhouettes and materials has created great admiration for his work and profitability for Burberry. Bailey has supported a variety of charitable projects through Burberry including the Fashion for Relief Initiative, and he serves as a mentor for young designers.

Diesel: Wilbert Das (1963–)

In 1988, Renzo Rosso hired Wilbert Das, who had just graduated from the Academy of Fine Arts in Arnhem, Holland. More than twenty years later, Das is still at Diesel as the creative director responsible for all visual aspects of the company. Das and Rosso have collaborated on innovative techniques to dye, distress, and shape denim that have made Diesel jeans distinct. Das has a quiet, relaxed approach to his work and has focused on building a successful team known for their collaborative, nurturing culture. Putting his energy into keeping himself and his team innovative has proven successful, allowing the company to support new talent including the International Talent Support event and the Diesel Wall project. With Rosso's proven eye for spotting new talent, this strategy should keep Diesel at the forefront of denim design.

Gap inc.: Patrick Robinson (1967–)

Gap Inc. has been in business for over forty years and through that time has had many different designers lead the brand. Patrick Robinson is the current executive vice president of design for Gap Adult and Gap Body. Both his high-end fashion and mass-market experience are considered assets to the brand. He has a grounded point of view and sees great value in bringing well-designed garments to the masses. Robinson's previous experience includes time as artistic director at Paco Rabanne in Paris, designer of a limited-edition collection for Target's GO International, senior designer roles at Perry Ellis and Anne Klein, and design director at Le Collezioni White Label by Giorgio Armani. Robinson's work reflects a strong understanding of American sportswear, with reference to adventure and a worldview. Robinson is an alumnus of the Parsons School of Design and was one of *Vogue* magazine's 100 rising stars in 1996. Robinson supports the (RED) campaign with Gap's (PRODUCT)RED clothing and the Global Fund, which helps women and children affected by AIDS in Africa.

Jil Sander: Raf Simons (1968–)

Raf Simons, creative director for women's wear and menswear at Jil Sander, began his career as a furniture designer following his education in industrial design. He launched his own fashion collection in 1995 and was head professor at Vienna's University of Applied Arts for five years. Simons's design aesthetic is in harmony with the simple, pristine design traditions of Jil Sander. He is an inventive designer and has been a strong but quiet influence in menswear, introducing the graphic pencil slim silhouette in the 1990s. His own menswear lines, Raf Simons and Raf by Raf Simons, are respected for their modern interpretations of shape and their lifestyle reflection of young men. His Jil Sander women's wear line is admired for his modern shapes designed for high-level career women, especially the pantsuit. Simons is sensitive to the emotions and needs of the individuals that he dresses and to the traditions of the house. His attention to world events and youth subcultures, music, and graphic art provides inspiration and a deep connection to modern life. In his recent collaboration with EastPack, Simons created a series of bags as part of his own Material World collection. He has also worked with Fred Perry, a British brand, to design a thirteen-piece menswear collection intended to broaden Fred Perry's audience.

Target inc.: design teams

Multiple brands are designed using a team approach under Target's internal brand labels. Target has a talented, diverse team of 300 product, textile, and technical designers who work with merchandisers to develop and drive the product assortment. It is a collaborative product-development approach, headed by divisional design directors and senior technical managers. Each design team researches and analyzes key trends, then selects the color story, key silhouettes, and overall "mood" for their brands. They then propose their ideas to the merchants. The design director works to guide the point of view and the point of difference for each line so that across the six divisions and multiple brands, Target presents a fresh, trend-right aesthetic. With their expertise on the guest segments and competitive market assortments, the division merchandisers lead their team from the business side. The technical-development team ensures optimal fit and develops the detail specifications for the factories. A smaller percentage of Target apparel is developed by outside brands, including Champion and Converse. These are very collaborative partnerships, and the Target design directors review the collections so that they fit the company's business and design objectives. Target's goal is to leverage the talents of all their employees, and the retailer uses shared goals, objectives, and rewards to drive the teams. Their culture can be described as one that values new ideas and drives innovation by creating balance between strategy and a focused need to increase the speed of development to meet the needs of their guests. Target is known and respected for giving 5 percent of its income to support education, the arts, and social services in the communities in which the retailer does business, along with countless volunteer hours. Target also has a commitment to environmental stewardship as a core practice of its business.

FASHION FOCUS FROM THE FIELD: LUELLA BARTLEY (1974–)

In 2006, Luella Bartley became part of retail history when she was the first fashion designer to do a collection for retail-chain Target's GO International program. The idea of a high-end fashion designer designing an affordable collection to be sold exclusively at a mass-market discounter was a new concept that became contagious in the market. Perhaps it was a strategic move for Bartley, who launched her first collection in London in 1999; her name is now recognized widely in the United Kingdom and the United States. Her style is viewed as effortless street chic that combines pretty girl punk with preppy undertones. Collaborations with Mulberry to design a line of bags and with Vans, Churches, Sony, and M.A.C. have successfully expanded her brand. Bartley has collaborated with Tonic, a do-good Web site, several times by designing T-shirts and bags to raise funds for nonprofit organizations that support the environment, education, social welfare, and reduction of poverty. She joined other designers including Vivienne Westwood to create a new collection of dresses inspired by Disney Princesses to be auctioned off for UNICEF.

Bartley's surfing and horseback-riding lifestyle appears carefree, even with three children, thus maintaining her young, fresh persona. Designing appears to be a better fit than her earlier positions as a journalist at the *Evening Standard* and British *Vogue*. A favorite in Milan and New York, she takes "The Luella Roadshow" to unusual venues. Her willingness to take risks supports her creative success and serves as a reminder that fashion is supposed to be fun.

Beyond apparel

All designers, regardless of the product that they design, are prepared to work with the same core of design elements. Color, line and form, drawings, and materials are a few of the basic design tools. Training as a designer develops an approach to thinking, working, and problem solving that creates diverse opportunities. Thus a skilled designer should be able to design a range of products and applications based on specific requirements. A clothing designer has the advantage of understanding how to design a three-dimensional object for the human body. Skills and knowledge are easily transferred to other product types with additional understanding of the new product, market, materials, and technology.

As fashion designers build their brands, expansion and growth are often achieved with the development of diverse product lines. Designers originally expanded into perfumes as a way to include those who aspired to a designer lifestyle but could not afford expensive clothing. The term *brand extension* is used to describe this process of expanding a brand name into another category of goods. The strategy has been applied to accessories, furniture, home products, cars, cell phones, and hotels, thus making a small part of the designer lifestyle available to the average consumer. When a designer or brand is well known, using the name on other products attracts consumers, who equate the product with the lifestyle represented by that designer.

The connection between the brand image and the new product can be very direct. For example, the Versace Medusa head, a motif used on apparel, has also been used on their line of dinnerware. Missoni's line of bed and bath textiles takes its inspiration from Missoni's fashion direction, and the textiles are easily identified as Missoni design. The connection can also be more abstract, capturing the mood and lifestyle of the brand without a direct connection to a distinct motif or original fashion inspiration. For example, Calvin Klein bedding is clean-lined and tailored, evoking the image of Calvin Klein; however, the consumer would not readily identify the bedding brand without the Calvin Klein name. Clean-lined and tailored could represent a variety of well-known designers. Furniture and home accessory companies have used high-profile names including Ralph Lauren, Oscar de la Renta, Fendi, Missoni, Vivienne Westwood, and Vera Wang to attract consumers who recognize their well-known styles.

Using a designer name creates a point of differentiation that allows the product to stand out among many choices. It can also provide a connection to a new group of consumers who may not be familiar with the original brand. For example, Marc Jacobs has done a collection of glassware and china for Waterford, and Monique Lhuillier, bridal wear designer, has worked with Royal Doulton to produce a line of fine china. Waterford and Royal Dalton are well-known names among a traditional, elite group of consumers. Adding the Jacobs and Lhuillier names updates the image of these two companies, making them appealing to a young, nontraditional group of consumers. In an effort to attract nontechie consumers, Zac Posen created a leather camera bag that accompanied a limited number of Nikon's Coolpix cameras. A designer name that is appealing to the desired audience of a nonclothing brand can create instant brand identity. The designer name has value because it connects the new product to the established brand image.

FASHION FOCUS FROM THE FIELD: TODD OLDHAM: RENAISSANCE DESIGNER (1961–)

His name might not be as well known as others, but Todd Oldham is an extraordinarily diverse designer who continues to be enthusiastic about many areas of design. He started as a fashion designer in New York, winning the CFDA Perry Ellis award in 1991, and as a commentator on MTV's *House of Style*. He is currently the design creative director for Old Navy. His work includes interior design, film, photography, furniture, graphic art, and a collection of floral designs for FTD.com. Oldham is known outside of fashion for a line of dorm room furnishings for Target and a line of furniture for La-Z-Boy. He is a mentor on the television show *Top Design* with a focus on interior design and is developing a television series called *Handmade Modern*. This interest in craft really returns to his roots: His family, particularly his grandmother, kept him busy with a variety of eclectic crafts while he was growing up. His design aesthetic is quirky and similar to Schiaparelli in spirit. Craft elements are a strong focus. He runs Todd Oldham Studio, a multifaceted, full-service design studio in New York, and has a devotion to accessible design. As an author and photographer he has published several books. Oldham has a spirit that is honest and playful and full of boundless creative energy, guaranteeing that his next project will be a surprise. He exemplifies the opportunities that are possible for all designers, regardless of their training.

A variety of creative and business agreements, either long or short term, can be developed between the designer and the new product collaborator depending on the needs of each party. The level of involvement with the actual design can also vary greatly, from the licensing of the designer's name with no direct involvement at one end of the continuum to a designer having complete control over development of new products. Actual practice tends to fall somewhere in the middle, with some design direction from the named designer but with other designers executing and supporting the new product concept.

Occasionally, a designer from outside the field of fashion begins to design apparel. Raf Simons, creative director at Jil Sander, began his career as a furniture designer and was trained in industrial design. Serena Williams, tennis champion, is designing sports apparel for Nike. A recent degree in fashion design makes her experience on the courts even more valuable, as she can develop products that support tennis performance and help grow the game.

Collaboration

Collaboration with another professional or a team is a natural way for designers to work. Reaching across domains often results in an idea or product that is innovative and unique because the development draws on the diverse strengths of those involved. Collaboration is also an outlet for designers to extend their thinking and creativity, providing a new perspective. Collaboration is not new: Paul Poiret was involved with the theater, interior design, and printing. Coco Chanel worked with theater and film projects. Elsa Schiaparelli had perhaps one of the most famous collaborations, with the artist Salvador Dali. She exhibited his artwork in her shopwindows to attract customers, and his ideas were translated into many of her designs, including the famous shoe-shaped hat and a tailored suit with drawers instead of pockets. Dali's artwork is seen on her Lobster dress and in the fabric design for the tear illusion dress that looks torn. He also designed the bottle for her fragrance Roi Soleil. This collaboration sets an excellent example. Both contributors bring their strengths to a project, which are well respected by the other, and proceed to encourage and challenge the partner.

Successful, modern collaborations continue to bring innovation to design. Marimekko founder Armi Ratia collaborated with architect Aarno Ruusuvuori in a modernism experiment in Finland. Marimekko, known for its clear, bright graphic textiles, was attracted to the austere work of Ruusuvuori, and together they conceived a utopian village for 3,500 inhabitants, including Marimekko employees. The minimum dwellings were pure in form and free of the dictates of previous generations, but unfortunately the concept was never realized due to economic factors and the rural location.

Architect Zaha Hadid designed a mobile exhibition pavilion for Chanel in collaboration with Karl Lagerfeld. Inspired by the iconic quilted Chanel bag, the ultralight, reflective building composed of continuously arching elements breaks down

Figure 5.6 Collaborators Elsa Schiaparelli and Salvador Dali. Image originally donated to Lorraine Evans to use on www.house-of-francheska.co.uk/ on a noncommercial basis. Original use of the image is for educational purposes only.

into pieces for easy transportation. Rem Koolhaas has worked on several buildings for Prada that experiment with using architecture to reinvent the retail experience. The Soho store in New York has a built-in ability to change in structure and appearance, and the Beverly Hills, California, store opens up directly to the street without a façade, inviting people to enter. Prada's store in Tokyo was designed by Herzog and de Meuron with a similar concept of ability to change but with a definite view to the outside city.

When the collaboration between a designer and another business partner is only on a cosmetic or superficial level, there is not much long-term value in the venture. However, when the collaboration between two designers involves shared goals, the results can be invaluable. Short-term business-only relationships may fade as a strategy for economic return; however, serious collaboration between designers should be supported as a long-term investment. Creative ideas flourish in an environment that values experimentation and risk and has a view toward the future.

Fashion and architecture

There has been increasing interest in the relationship between fashion and architecture that goes beyond building spaces for retail stores. Both fields use flat, two-dimensional materials to construct three-dimensional forms, despite the obvious difference in scale. Several museum exhibitions, Intimate Architecture:

Contemporary Clothing Design, at the Massachusetts Institute of Technology; The Fashion of Architecture: Constructing the Architecture of Fashion, at the Center for Architecture in New York; and Skin and Bones, at the Museum of Contemporary Art in Los Angeles, have explored this topic. Bradley Quinn searches for common elements in his book, *The Fashion of Architecture*.

Summary

- Innovative development and use of fabrics for apparel characterize Miyake, Prada, Ghesquière, and Loudermilk.
- Jacobs is a celebrity in the vein of the old couture but embraces the modern concept of teamwork.
- Fellow British designers McQueen, Westwood, and Hamnett are known for their witty, theatrical, political, and often shocking presentations intended to raise a voice for change. Van Noten is exceedingly true to his voice that rejects the call of fashion and values historic preservation.
- The Altruists have diverse design directions but share a common concern for others. Attention to spirituality and a focus on sensual interaction with their garments have provided direction for Karan and Yamamoto. McCartney is well known for her earth-friendly perspective and Johnson for her support of breast cancer research.
- The emerging talents of Lam, Panichgul, Kane, and the Mulleavys bring diverse and global perspectives to Western fashion.
- Solid training and apprenticeship in tailoring, draping, and technical design skills have given these designers a strong foundation to take leadership in fashion.
- These contemporary designers are confident in their vision and often described as rising above the trends.
- Anonymous designers behind the big brands provide creative direction without the need for a public persona.
- A strong designer uses an approach to thinking, working, and problem solving that is adaptive to a variety of design fields and projects.
- Collaborative design work has become an accepted and profitable approach in the market.

Vocabulary

- altruist
- apprentice
- collaborative
- brand extension
- modern
- mass market
- innovative
- timeless

Discussion

1. What are the qualities of a successful designer? Do you think that formal training is necessary?
2. What are the advantages and disadvantages of being a designer with your name as the brand versus being a name behind the brand?
3. Contrast the role of a couture designer with the role of a contemporary designer in Western fashion.
4. Do designers have a responsibility to do philanthropic work once their business is successful?
5. What should a designer consider before entering into a partnership or collaboration?
6. Why do so many designers suggest that their work doesn't follow the trends?
7. What do you think the future will be like for celebrity designers? Justify your response.

6

GLOBAL FASHION CENTERS

Fashion is practiced around the world. Fashion centers are unique cities supported by a variety of cultural and economic activities that create a system of information and ideas that support fashion innovation. As the quintessential fashion center, Paris offers a distinct urban culture of architecture, art, shopping, and daily life that embraces fashion as an essential element in the life of the people and the city. Haute couture made Paris the historical world center of fashion, and while haute couture remains the focus of Parisian fashion, a broader view of the world and fashion have allowed the development of many other fashion centers. Each city has a distinctive perception of fashion that reflects the individual people and place.

In addition to strong cultural and financial resources, traditional fashion centers required specialized manufacturing capabilities; a large, inexpensive labor force; and centers for shopping. The top five established fashion centers—London, Milan, New York, Paris, and Tokyo—were built on their economic and manufacturing strengths and their role in the world economy. Access to materials, capital, and ideas and the influx of people, both workers and consumers, made them powerful world cities as well as fashion centers. While they remain as such, the world has become smaller and more accessible due to improved communication and transportation technologies. Much of the manufacturing of apparel has moved out of these cities and into other, developing areas of the world.

The focus of these key cities and fashion centers has shifted to creating cultural economies and creative industries that are less labor-intensive. In place of producing tangible fashion apparel, the fashion center of the twenty-first century is becoming a hub for developing commodities of fashion knowledge. These new fashion cities are home to headquarters of global marketing, branding, and advertising along with the cultural commodities of music, film, and the arts. With the increased use of outsourcing to produce a city's apparel products, the role of these fashion centers is more focused on symbolic production of fashion. There is increasing opportunity for other, emerging world cities to become fashion centers: some in the model of the traditional fashion center and others in a new format.

Even as companies look globally to produce and sell their apparel products, the idea of globalization contradicts fashion. A globalized product or brand is one that is standardized for all consumers regardless of individual preferences or needs. This may work for a cell phone but is much harder to imagine for fashion apparel. The apparel industry is mainly comprised of small firms that have limited technology or economy-of-scale advantages and address a wide range of consumer tastes and needs. Most apparel is not really appropriate for globalization. A more polycentric view of global fashion that places value on the unique qualities of person and place reflected in the apparel supports the concept of more local product diversity, which would be available from multiple worldwide fashion centers. A distinct product identity based on local design characteristics distinguishes a garment from others in a global market that too often appears uniform. Individual consumers have the desire to purchase apparel from a global market but are looking for an individual experience, often rooted in place.

Fashion centers have been synonymous with key world cities; thus a thriving fashion community is often an indicator of a city's position in the world order. Vibrant urban centers that embrace local traditions and histories can produce an atmosphere of creativity that attracts attention and an influx of a wide variety of people, ideas, and attitudes. Creating a unique culture of design and commerce is a valuable resource for an aspiring fashion center. Though Shanghai has been called the Paris of the East and Buenos Aires is referred to as the Paris of South America, each must ultimately rely on its own qualities to establish itself as a fashion center. With the globalization of many shopping malls and retailers, the value of distinct shopping districts and streets translates into economic value for a city as a fashion center. Museums also influence the perception of a city as a fashion center by showcasing design traditions and cultural values. While the established Western fashion media play some role in directing the perceptions of a fashion center, many local governments and industry partners have invested significant resources to develop and promote themselves as fashion centers.

A true global fashion center in the twenty-first century must still have a strong core of economic and cultural resources that support creative innovation, along with a trained network of employees and entrepreneurs. Building a distinct environment that can become an original voice among growing global fashion is a challenge and an opportunity for many cities. The following, organized by continent, presents current fashion centers and those cities that are actively reaching to achieve that status, with a brief history of how the city became a fashion center and how it maintains that role.

Asia

Tokyo

Tokyo's development as an international fashion center advanced rapidly following the success of designers Hanae Mori, Kenzo Takada, and Issey Miyake in Paris during the 1970s. The foundation for this advancement started in the early twentieth century as the Japanese slowly began to adopt Western-style dress for daily wear, reserving the kimono for special occasions. Bunka Fashion College educated students and the public about Western dress, publishing Japan's first fashion magazine, *So-en*, beginning in 1936 and preparing students to work in the ready-to-wear industry following World War II. A signature Tokyo style that used traditional Japanese shapes and techniques for constructing Western clothing began to emerge, creating a new aesthetic that captured world attention when Japanese designers began to show in Paris. The 1980s look of Rei Kawakubo of Comme des Garçons and Yohji Yamamoto advanced the style, presenting a radically different avant-garde approach to dressing that used deconstructed forms that hid the body to create an original statement. Very trendy, cute, high-quality character brands became popular in the Japanese markets at this time as well. These teen street-fashion brands included Pink House, MILK, and Jane Marple. Japan experienced high economic growth during the 1980s, and people were eager to experiment with clothes. The founding of the Council of Fashion Designers, Tokyo, in 1985 eventually led to the first Japan Fashion Week in 2005 with support from the Japanese government and local designers.

Casual fashion took over in the 1990s as a result of an economic downturn, and Tokyo street fashion began to draw international attention as a fresh interpretation of casual fashion. Shibuya and Harajuku were the first areas of the city to exhibit teenage fashion trends including Lolita, Kogal, Ganguro, and Bosozoku. These trends continue to change quickly, stimulating purchases, original designs, and continued international interest. *Wired* magazine has a regular Japanese Schoolgirl Watch feature. Street fashion has launched practicing designers including Jun Takahashi, designer of Under Cover, who originated from the Ura Hara area of Harajuku and later showed collections in Paris.

Creative innovation extends throughout Tokyo fashion, with its fabric advancements in engineering and design making its textile manufacturers some of the most respected in the world. Miyake developed an innovative technique for producing permanently pleated fabric based on traditional Shibori techniques for his Pleats Please line. His concept for A-Poc (A Piece of Cloth) lets an individual cut out a custom-designed garment from a knitted piece of fabric, allowing the wearer to decide on the final form. For example, the neckline shape or hem length is easily altered, or a hat or tights can emerge from the cloth by cutting along a variety of predetermined style lines. Designer Yoshiki Hishinuma continues to develop original, wearable fabrics and designs using the power of technology and a creative mind.

Tokyo has a strong reputation for high-quality manufacturing and creative design that balances tradition and innovation, and a customer base that makes up one of the largest luxury markets in the world. The Japanese's fondness of international brands is well known, and they make up one of the largest international markets for luxury products. However, Tokyo still struggles with attracting international wholesale buyers for local Japanese fashion.

Figure 6.1 Tokyo, 2009, courtesy of Karen LaBat.

Consumers and visitors shop in the following areas of the city: Shibuya is a major shopping area that attracts teens and young adults; Harajuku is a welcoming area with high-end and uniquely Japanese boutiques; Shinjuku has fashion malls with higher-end boutiques with both international and local designers; Nakameguro is the center for retro, vintage, and street fashion; Daikanyama provides shopping for the more mature customer with Japanese and international designer stores; Aoyama is a trendy high-fashion area with many brand-name and designer stores; Takeshita-dori represents the cutting edge of fashion in Tokyo; Omotesando is the center of world fashion consumption with high-end international boutiques; and Ginza houses Tokyo's oldest and most prestigious department stores, including the exclusive Wako. The best local inspirations for designers include the Bunka Gakuen Costume Museum, the Edo Tokyo Museum, and the Tokyo Metropolitan Teien Art

Museum; however, the city is filled with a great diversity of museums that represent the cultural, historical, and scientific interests of the city.

Shanghai

Shanghai has been China's city of style since the late nineteenth century. The city was the center of foreign trade, which provided access to imported textiles and new ideas that supported constant change. It was also the center of the publishing industry, which reported on Western fashion news, as well as a hub of the film industry. Skilled tailors and large department stores that promoted their merchandise supported a population with an intense appreciation of fashion. Fashion essentially stopped after World War II, but a small production industry and tailoring expertise survived. When the People's Republic of China was established, more goods became available for export, primarily to other Communist countries. Though fashion was considered frivolous during the Cultural Revolution from 1966 to 1976, the Chinese found subtle ways to individualize the utilitarian style of their clothing. Fashion was suppressed, but citizens were required by the state to pay careful attention to a respectful appearance.

Once reform occurred and China's economy began growing in the 1980s, people began to pay attention to fashion again and Shanghai was ready to resume its position as China's fashion center. Shanghai is very image conscious and proud of its fashion reputation. With a strong financial district, a metropolitan infrastructure, and port access, the government is now promoting Shanghai as an international fashion center: the Paris of the East. International brands are in demand, and a growing number of local designers are reviving Shanghai's status. There have been great efforts to promote Chinese fashion, mainly to European buyers. Designer Xie Feng, China's first designer to show a ready-to-wear collection in Paris, presented his label, Jefen, during the 2007 Spring Fashion Week. That same fall, Karl Lagerfeld staged an extravagant runway show for Fendi on the Great Wall of China. Ma Ke introduced her ready-to-wear line in the following years and in 2008 was the first Chinese designer invited to show during the Paris couture shows. With a stark aesthetic that rejects fast-fashion trends, Ma Ke is one of the most important emerging fashion designers in China.

The Shanghai International Fashion Cultural Festival has been an annual event since 1995 and brings together industry, designers, and academia for a month of related events and contests that provide high visibility. Students from top institutions including the China Academy of Art, Beijing Institute of Fashion Technology, National Dong Hwa University, and Suzhou University compete for recognition. Shanghai remains the media center for fashion magazines and television, though manufacturing occurs in smaller areas outside the city and in the southeastern region of China.

The Shanghai Museum of Art provides inspiration from ancient cultures, but shopping, not sightseeing, is the main attraction in Shanghai. The Huaihai/French Concession houses international flagship stores and shopping malls; Nanjing Lu is

Figure 6.2 Out Side In collection, a collaboration between Michael Esson, professor at the University of New South Wales, Australia, and Peng Bo, professor at Donghua University, presented at the 2009 Donghua Fashion Week, part of the Shanghai International Fashion Culture Festival, courtesy of Juan Juan Wu.

the main shopping street with a variety of fashion, malls, and traditional crafts; Shi Liu Pu cloth market is a center for skilled tailors; Xujiahui is a developing retail area with malls and large department stores focused on Western brands; Yuyuan Garden is a market with traditional handicrafts; and Xintiandi is an urban area with restaurants, bars, and shops in restored traditional-style Shikumen houses.

Bangkok

Apparel and textiles are the largest manufacturing industry in Thailand. In the late 1980s, apparel production companies began to develop and expanded rapidly. At this time, the Thai industry started to think strategically about the growth of Thai fashion for the local market, the tourist trade, and export. The Thailand Textile Institute helps companies compete in the global marketplace by sharing information on production issues, such as labor and social welfare protection, environmental protection, product safety, and efficiency. Thailand's strength is in addressing the higher-quality, lower-volume needs of niche markets. Though Thai silk and textiles have an international reputation for quality, the city's creative potential, innovative spirit, and appreciation for the ancient and the modern are not as well known. The desire to make Bangkok a fashion center is strong; however, the direction and vision for developing the fashion component are weak.

With a strong tourist industry and local Thai consumers who have an increasing interest in international fashion, retail has grown beyond the traditional street market. In 1997, the first luxury mall, Emporium Shopping Complex, opened and became a destination for local and international shoppers. Small fashion events also began to occur to introduce the concept of Thailand as a fashion center, and soon Siam Paragon, another luxury shopping complex, was opened. Some leaders in the fashion industry convinced the government to support the development of Thailand as a fashion center, but the national policy lasted only a short time. Bangkok International Fashion Week has continued as a twice-a-year event, and the Ministry

Figure 6.3 Siam Paragon Shopping Center, Bangkok, 2009, courtesy of Karen LaBat.

of Commerce hosts the Bangkok International Fashion Fair and Bangkok International Leather Fair to showcase Thai designers. Brands such as Fly Now, Greyhound, and Senada have international recognition, and others are working toward that goal. The potential for Bangkok to become a fashion center still exists, but efforts to promote and support Thai fashion have been fragmented, even with their strong apparel production industry.

Designers and tourists can choose from a wide variety of shopping, from outdoor markets to high-end luxury malls in Bangkok. Siam Paragon is a shopping mall for luxury goods; Sukhumvit Road is home to high-end stores and unique boutiques; Mah Boon Krong (MBK) Shopping Center is where locals and tourists shop; the Emporium is a luxury mall with three floors of fashion; the Gaysorn complex is a marble and chrome high-end shopping complex with international and Thai designers; and Chatuchat market is the city's largest outdoor market. Bangkok offers inspiration from many cultural, religious, and historic sites including the Grand Palace, the Temple of the Reclining Buddha, and the Erawan Shrine. The National Gallery provides a look at Thai art.

New Delhi

Vibrant colors; beautiful, embellished silks; and the sari represent part of India's rich fashion culture. This culture has developed over thousands of years, but only in the late twentieth century did New Delhi begin to emerge as an international fashion center. India's cotton and silk resources, skilled workers, and low labor costs support New Delhi's role as India's main fashion city. Located in the northern region of India, it is the capital city and home to many fashion and textile schools as well as the Fashion Design Council of India (FDCI). International promotion of Indian fashion and establishment of a fashion district in New Delhi are current goals of the FDCI. *Indian Vogue*, based in New Delhi, debuted in September 2007 and should help promote Indian designers, photographers, and models.

There is some rising fashion competition from the city of Mumbai, which is growing as a financial and cultural center and the heart of India's film industry, Bollywood. Younger designers have been attracted to Mumbai, and they have launched a competing fashion week. According to the *Global Language Monitor* ("Top Fashion Cities," 2008), a source that counts words in global media outlets, Mumbai leads New Delhi as a top fashion city because it has a higher number of references to fashion. It will be important to monitor the growth and development of these two cities.

The first India Fashion Week in New Delhi was held in 2000, though the foundation was laid by Jeannie Naoroji, who organized the first India fashion show in 1958. Traditional styles of Indian dress that focused on wrapped and custom-made garments have transitioned to a growing prêt-à-porter fashion industry. Individually and collectively, Indian designers are striving to develop a signature style that combines

Figure 6.4 Fashion display at India's largest retailer, Globus, 2007, courtesy of Sandra Evenson.

their rich textile traditions with an aesthetic and silhouette that have global appeal. Several Indian designers are becoming known internationally; these include Kumar Ahmed, who gives an Indian aesthetic to tailored silhouettes; Manish Arora, who has shown in Paris and is known as the John Galliano of India; and Gaurav Gupta, who highlights Indian fabrics in his Western cuts. While international buyers and investors are looking for new talent, there is concern that many designers lack a strong focus and have weak technical skills, and that the infrastructure to support production is not yet firmly established. The majority of sales during fashion week have been to domestic buyers interested in a more traditional style.

New Delhi was established in the sixth century but has all the energy of any modern city. Shopping ranges from historic markets to high-end boutiques and includes Chandni Chowk, an old wholesale market; Connaught Place, the city's main shopping area; Santushti Shopping Arcade and Khan Market, which provide high-end, independent boutique shopping; Lajpat Nagar and Dili Haat markets, which focus on artisan crafts and fabrics; Mehrauli, home to India's best designers; and Gurgaon, which has many Western-style malls. Along with the local culture and history of New Delhi, the National Museum, the Crafts Museum, and the nearby Taj Mahal are rich sources of inspiration for designers.

North America

New York

New York was a manufacturing center and a city of immigrants at the start of the twentieth century. The city grew as a financial center, attracting individuals with an interest in culture and the arts. These elements provided the foundation for New York to become a thriving fashion center. Paris had been the main city of fashion, providing inspiration for New York manufacturers, who copied its designs. Change began to occur during World War II when inspiration from Paris was no longer available and the New York apparel industry began to look for local talent. Parsons School of Design provided trained employees, and the Fashion Institute of Technology was established in 1944 to address this need. Leading women in the fashion industry established the Fashion Group International in 1931 to promote the industry and the careers of women. They made connections across New York's retail businesses, the fashion press, the apparel and cosmetic industry, and cultural establishments that nurtured the development of New York City as a fashion center. A garment district around Seventh Avenue, now referred to as Fashion Avenue, was established, allowing manufacturers, suppliers, trade organizations, distributors, and retailers to operate in close proximity, facilitating communication and reducing costs.

New York fashion shows, awards, and special events were publicized internationally, and the city became known for sportswear, an original style of dress that reflected the more casual, relaxed lifestyle of American women. Ready-to-wear sportswear manufacturers were thriving, but the social and economic changes of the 1960s increased the demand for more individualized styles of dress. Designers moved from anonymous employees of a manufacturer to more prominence as they established their own companies. The desire for individuality directed the new practice of creating a distinct image for the designer, the product, and the consumer, who aspired to become part of the brand lifestyle (Rantisi, 2006). Bill Blass, Ralph Lauren, and Calvin Klein were pioneers in developing the concept of fashion lifestyle branding. Thus New York was well prepared to support the increased role of marketing and commerce in the fashion industry.

At the start of the twenty-first century, New York's role as a fashion center continues to change. The once-famous Garment District has lost manufacturers and many supporting businesses to global production, though Seventh Avenue remains a center for designing and marketing. The merger or loss of many established retailers has created a different business dynamic and a loss of independent perspectives. However, the financial and cultural elements that helped to establish New York as a fashion center remain and continue to offer opportunity for those who want to experience and communicate the vitality and original qualities of the city. Similar to Paris, New York has also become a fashion center that can provide validation for new designers. For example, Miuccia Prada became successful in Milan and internationally after establishing herself in New York.

New York's shopping and retail centers contribute to its reputation as a fashion center. They include the following: Brooklyn has small shops for both the hip and sophisticated; the East Village offers independent boutiques, vintage, and local designers; the Lower East Side is famous for concept boutiques, streetwear, and vintage shops; the Meatpacking District has become home to lifestyle boutiques and boasts a popular nightlife; Midtown/the Upper East Side is home to the famous Madison Avenue and Fifth Avenue department stores and designer flagships; Nolita has European-style specialty boutiques and higher-end local and international designers; SoHo is a mix of major labels and midmarket stores; Union Square and Flatiron offer major chain stores and streetwear; and the West Village is known for niche boutiques and accessories.

Inspiration for designers in the city comes from the international mix of residents and visitors and its vibrant cultural, political, and economic center of activities. In addition to the theater and music available in the city, there are a range of museums with fashion and textile collections. These include the Metropolitan Museum of Art fashion collection, which includes global dress and textiles; the Smithsonian Cooper-Hewitt National Design Museum for product design, decorative arts, and textiles; the Fashion Institute of Technology Museum with costumes and textiles of the twentieth century; and the Cora Ginsberg Gallery with eighteenth- and nineteenth-century costumes as well as textiles from the seventeenth century.

Los Angeles

Los Angeles is a fashion center that embraces two diverse sides of fashion. Los Angeles became a source of fantasy fashion as a result of Hollywood's glamorous movies, television, and the entertainment industry. From Adrian and Edith Head to Bob Mackie and Nolan Miller, Hollywood designers create garments seen in media around the world that influence fashion. In contrast, the California lifestyle of sun, surf, and active outdoor recreation represents a very casual, relaxed side of fashion. Both focus on the ideal of youth.

Los Angeles is an increasingly diverse city with a large immigrant population and financial resources from international trade, entertainment, and a strong manufacturing sector. Local schools including the California State University, Los Angeles, and the Fashion Institute of Design and Merchandising provide trained employees. These factors support the Los Angeles fashion district as the center of the fashion industry on the west coast of the United States, with apparel and textile manufacturers, retailers, and suppliers.

Los Angeles is well known for its retail and vintage shopping and is a popular travel destination for designers seeking inspiration. The primary shopping areas of the city include Abbot Kinney for independent boutiques; Beverly Hills, with Rodeo Drive and Wilshire Boulevard housing international designer flagships and high-end department stores; Echo Park and downtown for independent boutiques, designers, and vintage; the Fairfax District for skate and hip-hop; Los Feliz with more independent boutiques and vintage; Melrose Heights for international designer boutiques and designer vintage; Robertson Boulevard with trendy boutiques; Santa Monica for midmarket retail and independent boutiques; Sunset Plaza with international and American designer boutiques; and West 3rd Street with independent, eclectic designers and boutiques. Museums including the Los Angeles County Museum of Art, the Museum of Contemporary Art, and the Getty Center can provide inspiration for designers. However, the entertainment, the climate, and the lifestyle have the greatest impact on Los Angeles as a fashion center.

FASHION FOCUS FROM THE FIELD: CHICAGO

While Chicago does not have a reputation as a big fashion center, the city is well positioned to take advantage of the new trend toward locally produced fashion. The third-largest city in the United States, Chicago is a major transportation and telecommunications hub and a major business, financial, and industrial center. Currently, more than 250 designers take advantage of the architecture, culture, and diversity of this vibrant city. Many designers feel that the city allows them to be more experimental with their designs without the pressures of a big fashion center. The designers are interested in expanding production facilities, as most want the advantages of manufacturing locally. The Chicago Fashion Foundation was established as a professional networking organization with the goal of promoting Chicago's fashion industry worldwide. It coordinates education for the fashion community and provides academic scholarships for local students.

Chicago has a long tradition of fashionable retail, tracing the history of Marshall Field's, now Macy's, to 1852. Macy's strategy of differentiating its stores supports the sale of local designer lines in its State Street location. It embraces the new Chicago Fashion Council's efforts to boost awareness of and promote Chicago's fashion industry. Perhaps the biggest boost for Chicago fashion is that local designer Maria Pinto is one of the first lady Michelle Obama's favorite designers. This midwestern city appears poised to become a model for a new fashion center with a local focus.

Toronto

As the largest city in Canada, Toronto is the center of Canadian fashion and one of the most diverse cities in the world. From a history of Hudson Bay blankets and Canuck culture, Toronto has built a reputation for style, innovation, and strong design and manufacturing. Holt Renfrew, a high-end retailer, has supported fashion in the city since 1889. The visibility of the city increased internationally during the 1970s with the establishment of the Roots brand and the start of the Toronto Film Festival. The center of the fashion district is in the King-Spadina neighborhood, originally home to diverse groups of immigrants who provided much-needed labor. Currently,

Toronto has a vibrant advertising and successful fashion publishing industry and is home to *FashionTV*, the only 24/7 coverage of fashion, lifestyle, and trends with worldwide distribution. Toronto Fashion Week occurs biannually, and the Festival of Architecture and Design takes place every May to showcase Toronto's broader support of design.

Toronto supports its fashion industry with programs by the Matinee Limited Fashion Foundation, which provides financial assistance to designers who are in the early stages of starting their businesses, and the Fashion Incubator, a nonprofit organization supported by the Fashion Industry Liaison Committee of Toronto to help new designers trying to launch their business. Students from Ryerson University and Sheridan College have strong contacts with Toronto's fashion industry. Many designers, including Linda Lundström, take inspiration from Canada's native people and traditional forms of dress for the northern climate, showcasing Canada's resources, including fur. Other designers, from David Dixon to Nada Shepherd, represent a more cosmopolitan side of fashion influenced by the diversity of cultures in the city and a strong awareness of the world.

Toronto's main fashion retail areas include Bloor-Yorkville, the main shopping area with designer boutiques, department stores, and mass-market flagships; Queen Street West, which begins with trendy youth shops and then transitions into independent boutiques; and Kensington Market, which provides vintage finds and outlets for beginning designers. Toronto provides other inspiration at the Royal Ontario Museum with the Patricia Harris Gallery of Textiles and Costume, the Bata Shoe Museum, and the Textile Museum of Canada.

Europe

Paris

Fashion's first city is Paris. As the home of haute couture, Paris's history is intertwined with the history of modern Western fashion. Paris has been a center of intellectual and artistic achievement for centuries, giving the city a personality and charm unlike any other. Dressing well is part of Parisian culture, and historically women worldwide have looked to Frenchwomen as style icons. Louis XIV, Marie Antoinette, and Empress Eugénie had the influence to set the fashions in Europe; thus Parisian tailors and dressmakers built a reputation as the world's best. With a renowned luxury-textile industry and a large immigrant population, the French invested in educating and training a multitude of skilled designers, seamstresses, embroiderers, button makers, and accessory craftspeople.

Fashion is respected as a serious business in France; thus, there is strong regulation and support by the government to protect its second-largest industry for its economic and tourist value. Because Paris is so supportive of its designers, it attracts talented young designers from around the world who hope to be recognized on the runway and in the press. Acceptance to show at Paris Fashion Week is a point of validation for rising designers who have included Kenzo, Miyake, Prada, and Galliano. When an international designer from India, Shanghai, or the United States makes a debut in Paris, it becomes career-making news. Though the haute couture business has been greatly reduced, the thousands of dollars needed to maintain the elite houses and produce the lavish fashion shows are still seen as an important investment. The prestige they create for the city and the benefits gained for the prêt-à-porter and accessory lines keep the fashion tradition alive. Today Paris continues its role as the leader of high fashion, coexisting with other international fashion centers: each with a unique offering.

Shopping in Paris is world famous; important areas include Saint Germain, an elegant area of designer boutiques and shoes; the rue Saint Honoré and rue du Faubourg Saint Honoré for upscale brand-name shopping; the "golden triangle" of the Champs Elysées, Avenue George V, and Avenue Montaigne for high-end designer boutiques; the Jardin du Palais Royal for designer boutiques; Etienne Marcel and Les Halles for streetwear and vintage; Marais for one-of-a-kind boutiques and vintage; and Canal Saint Martin with its extraordinary bohemian boutiques. The Galeries Lafayette, Printemps, and Le Bon Marché department stores have a strong presence in the city.

Figure 6.5 The Champs Elysées, Paris, photographer David Niblack.

The ambiance of the city has traditionally provided inspiration for artists, and there are many cultural and historic venues to visit. Those specific to fashion and textiles include the Musée de la Mode et du Textile at the Louvre, an extensive textiles and costume collection; the Musée Galliera-Musée de la Mode de la Ville de Paris, for the history of fashion from the eighteenth century to the present; the Paris Institut Français de la Mode, a library and collection; the Bibliothèque Forney for decorative and fine arts; the Musée des beaux arts et de la dentelle, located in Calais, for the history of lace making; the Musée de l'Impression Sur Etoffes, located in Mulhouse, which has an extensive collection of printed textiles; and the Musée du Chapeau, Chazelles-su, located in Lyon, for hats from the eighteenth century to the present day.

Milan

Milan is known for fashion because it is synonymous with the Italian prêt-à-porter industry. Italy had a rich cultural history for luxury, particularly in textiles, leather, jewelry, and shoes, but lacked a central fashion focus until the early 1950s. Milan's current status is due in part to the efforts of a Florentine businessman, Giovan Battista Giorgini, who brought U.S. buyers to his home to see Italian designer collections. His success created the visibility Italian designers needed to succeed. Roman designers were also trying to create international visibility but chose to show their couture designs against the architecture of their city. However, Florence and Rome could not provide the Italian fashion industry with the geographic, industrial, or economic support of Milan. As a financial center with a strong history of design, a textile- and garment-manufacturing industry, and a view toward the international market, Milan became the center of prêt-à-porter for women's wear and menswear in the 1970s. Demand for the work of designers Giorgio Armani, Versace, and Missoni resulted from marketing a concept of luxury products that were more accessible and comfortable. A "Made in Italy" label became an indication of the highest level of quality, fashion, and craftsmanship.

Professionals in the supporting fashion areas of journalism, photography, television, and marketing were readily available in Milan, and textile and fashion associations were established to support the industry. The Camera Nazionale della Moda Italiana is responsible for managing the shows during Milan Fashion Week at the Milano Fashion Center. In the twenty-first century, Milan is renewing its effort to maintain the image of Milan as a fashion center. Demand for fast fashion and the expiration of the Multifiber Agreement in 2005, which limited the amounts that a developing country could export to a developed country, represent a changing consumer and a very different world market. Competition from an increase in lower-priced products from China and pressure to produce offshore have forced the Milanese to reconsider what differentiates Italian fashion. According to the *Global Language Monitor* ("Top Fashion Cities," 2008), Rome leads Milan as a top fashion city. A unified promotion of Italian fashion, Life in I Style, that brings together Rome for high fashion, Milan for prêt-à-porter, Florence for menswear, and Naples for tailoring may be the best way to ensure the strength of the apparel industry across the country. The perception of Italy as a country of elegance that is delighted with the simple pleasures of life continues.

In Milan, Italian and international designer stores are found on the Via Montenapoleone, Via della Spiga, Via Sant'Andrea, Via Manzoni, Via Borgospesso, and Via Santo Spirito. There is also a growing artisan-craft community returning some innovation and creativity to the city. The Città della Moda, or the City of Fashion, is planned as a central location in Milan to showcase fashion with a combination of commercial buildings, residences, schools, and shops.

London

London stands out as having an ideal mix of traditional and modern sensibilities. Though its reputation as a modern fashion center began in the 1960s, London has been the center of international market activity for much of its history due to strong roots as a world political and economic leader. Today, with over 250 museums, a thriving theater district, and a diverse population, the city is permeated with culture. Historically, the value of design and technology was elevated during the Great Exhibition of 1851, in an event that displayed Great Britain's readiness to lead in the development of industry that supported fashion and design for a growing society of consumers (Auerbach, 1999). London's historical standing as a leader in menswear and tailored garments was established through the excellence of the Savile Row bespoke tailors and local resources for high-quality wool textiles. Beau Brummell, an early nineteenth-century British socialite, is still the quintessential reference to an impeccably dressed gentleman. The British royalty have influenced fashion for centuries. Hardy Amies, a Savile row tailor and couturier, was Queen Elizabeth's dressmaker from 1955 to 1990 and helped develop her personal style. Princess Diana made a significant impact on fashion during her life. Her style was copied worldwide, and her support of British designers contributed to London's modern reputation as a fashion center.

London street fashion first exploded as the youth movement gained momentum in the late 1950s. Mary Quant, Biba's Barbara Hulanicki, Marion Foale, and Sally Tuffin designed clothes with simple shapes and bright colors that appealed to teens and young adults. The sexual and political revolution of the period was captured in London's music and fashion. Designers in Paris and the United States looked to London for inspiration that would move fashion into a new era. Jon Bates, who designed for the label Jean Varon, had a great impact on how the masses dressed with his affordable, must-have dresses. Zandra Rhodes began printing textiles specifically for the dresses she was designing in the early 1980s, and her business has continued into the twenty-first century. With a style influenced by India, Africa, and Turkey, Rifat Ozbek captured a youth market with a preference for the nightlife and the outrageous.

The British Fashion Council (BFC) was established in 1983 to support British designers and develop London's position as an international fashion center. Vivienne Westwood's origins as a designer for punk bands in the 1970s led her to the honor of British Designer of the Year in 1990, and her influence in fashion continues today. Alexander McQueen received the support of the BFC and was part of the newest generation of London designers, who include John Galliano, Matthew Williamson, Stella McCartney, and Alice Temperley. London colleges—Central Saint Martins, the Royal College of Art, and London College of Fashion—have a strong reputation for graduating innovative fashion designers. The BFC organizes the biannual London Fashion Week that provides international visibility for an apparel industry worth over £40 billion (approximately US$60 billion).

Figure 6.6 Issey Miyake Exhibit at the Victoria and Albert Museum, London, 2001, courtesy of E. Bye.

London's shopping and retail areas contribute to making London an international fashion center and popular tourist attraction. Local retailers including Harrod's, Selfridges, and Topshop are recognized globally. From high-end designer boutiques to outdoor markets, the main areas include South Kensington to Knightsbridge, a central shopping area with Harrod's and Harvey Nichols; Knightsbridge to Sloane Square for major fashion labels; Carnaby Street with independent stores, street fashion, and vintage; Oxford Street with Selfridges, Marks & Spencer, and international chain and discount stores; Spitalfields Market for an eclectic mix of crafts; and St. Christopher's Place for intimate independent and designer outlets.

London supports a wealth of wonderful cultural and historic venues. Of particular interest are the Victoria and Albert Museum for its world-famous fashion collection from the seventeenth century to today; the British Museum; the Tate British and International Modern Art Museum; the Crafts Council Library and archive of historical and contemporary craft; and, outside London in Bath, the Museum of Costume/Fashion Research Centre.

South America

Buenos Aires

Buenos Aires, Argentina, has the most vibrant design industry in South America and was named the "city of design" by the United Nations Educational, Scientific and Cultural Organization (UNESCO) in 2005. Often called the Paris of South America, the city has a reputation for nurturing the arts and innovative style and for producing high-quality leather goods. Its people have a creative energy: Their enjoyment of life and appreciation of the past support an aesthetic tradition with European roots. The government and many industry leaders are working to make Buenos Aires a fashion center. There is a strong textile and manufacturing sector and a growing number of talented designers. International media coverage of Buenos Aires Fashion Week has increased visibility. Top fashion firms include Jazmin Chebar, Tramando, and Wanama.

Buenos Aires' status as an international shopping destination is due to the high style, quality, and glamour of its retail venues. Alvear Avenue, in the Recoleta neighborhood, showcases European designers as well as the top local designers. It has been compared to New York's Fifth and Madison Avenues, Paris's Champs Elysées, and London's Oxford Street. Palermo Soho has high-quality independent and designer boutiques and leather goods.

Art museums in the city include the Museo de Arte Latinoamericano de Buenos Aires, with the works of Latin American artists; the Museo de Arte Popular José Hernández, which honors the Argentinian gaucho; the Museo Nacional de Arte Decorativo; and the Museo Nacional de Bellas Artes, which has an excellent collection of nineteenth- and twentieth-century Argentinean art.

Figure 6.7 Buenos Aires Fashion Week, 2008, courtesy of Dave Hiti.

São Paulo

São Paulo, Brazil, is another growing international fashion center. It is the largest city in South America, with a strong financial center and a promising sense of resourcefulness and imagination. Designers in São Paulo and Rio de Janeiro are making strong connections in Europe and the United States, with a focus on ethical and sustainable fashion. Melissa is known for eco-footwear, and Marcia Ganem's designs use recycled tires and seat belts. Daniella Helayel's popular dress line, Issa, captures the bright colors of Brazil without the flamboyance usually associated with Latin American design. The international visibility of Brazilian supermodel Gisele Bündchen has also drawn attention to Brazil. The main shopping area in São Paulo is Jardins with a range of Brazilian and international stores, and the elegant Daslu department store. The mix of cultures in the city supports a thriving variety of arts, including the Museu de Arte Moderna de São Paulo, the Museu de Arte de São Paulo, and the Pinacoteca do Estado.

Australia

As the largest producer and exporter of wool, Australia was a center for apparel manufacturing until the 1960s when new design talent began to emerge. Designers such as Prue Acton, who started her company in 1963 with a range (line) of young boutique dresses, and Trent Nathan, who designed women's wear and menswear, helped to establish Australian fashion. Carla Zampatti, known for her sophisticated fashion-forward women's wear, and Joseph Saba, who introduced Staggers jeans, were also part of emerging Australian fashion, and they continue to design today. Australian fashion is known for its use of beautiful, lightweight wools, vibrant colors, indigenous-inspired textiles, and a relaxed attitude. Influences are derived from a combination of the beach, an outdoor lifestyle, and the excitement of the country's urban cities. The city of Melbourne is the cultural and creative center with a long tradition of apparel production. Sydney's beach traditions are undergoing a cultural shift as the city adopts a more urban attitude. Both will play an important role in the future of Australian fashion.

Melbourne's Flinders Lane is the original hub of the apparel industry. Originally a manufacturing center that thrived with immigrant labor, the fashion culture of Melbourne has grown around the Melbourne Cup, a very fashionable horse race established in 1861. One of the most popular events on race day continues to be Fashions on the Field, when awards and prizes are given to the best-dressed woman and man. The Fall Australian Fashion Week, started in 1996, is held in Melbourne, and Sydney holds the complementary Spring Rosemont Australian Fashion Week. The Melbourne Fashion Festival held in March includes shows, exhibits, and industry events.

The Central Business District in Melbourne has Australian retailers, department stores, designer brands, and boutiques; Fitzroy offers streetwear and vintage; Prahan/Armadale is home to Chapel Street, with a wide range of retail; and Armadale is the area for upscale shopping. Inspiration from the arts can be found at the Ian Potter Centre for indigenous art, the Australian Centre for Contemporary Art, the National Gallery of Victoria with its excellent art collections, and Craft Victoria for contemporary design.

Sydney is best known for its swimwear and surf wear, with the most famous company being Speedo, started in 1928 by Alexander MacRae. Other internationally known brands include Roxy, Billabong, Rip Curl, and Seafolly. Sydney is home to many other internationally known designers including Akira Isogawa, who designs soft, romantic women's wear; Collette Dinnigan, the first Australian designer to show in Paris; Sass & Bide, who do several lines of innovative denim; and Jenny Kee, known for her bold colored knitwear.

The central business district in Sydney offers retail from midmarket to designer; Paddington has boutiques and galleries; Woollahra has upscale women's wear; Darlinghurst is known for streetwear; and Surry Hills has a creative, bohemian feel with boutiques and galleries. In addition to the beach and city, inspiration can be found at the Museum of Contemporary Art and the Art Gallery of New South Wales for Aboriginal art.

Africa

The fashion industry in Africa has the potential to bring original design to the international market but faces many challenges, including a lack of business skills and investors and the poor quality of local mass production. The African Fashion International group has been working on marketing and promotion of designers, with fashion weeks in Cape Town, Durban, and Johannesburg. Capetown has the largest concentration of up-and-coming designers and a developing infrastructure for manufacturing. The natural beauty and culture of Africa are rich and highly distinctive resources for designers. The first Africa fashion magazine television series was launched in 2008 to promote and recognize African fashion with the goal of improving the quality of fashion design from Africa. South Africa's best-known designer is Gavin Rajah, whose women's wear is shown internationally. He is a strong ambassador for African fashion and collaborated with South African Tourism in Paris to bring four emerging designers to show in the 2007 Paris Fashion Week. They included Thabani Mavundla, Thula Sindi, Craig Jacobs, and David Tlale. Retail in Capetown offers V&A Waterfront, a high-end shopping mall with local designers and independent boutiques; Cavendish Square with designer boutiques; Long Street for hip boutiques and vintage; and Kloof Street for boutiques and midmarket shops.

Additional fashion cities

Fashion thrives in many other cities. They deserve mention even though they are not currently on a trajectory toward becoming global fashion centers. Antwerp is a city that supports designers and has a history of lace making and textile manufacturing. The Royal Academy of Fine Arts has a reputation for producing original concept designers such as Dries Van Noten and Walter Van Beirendonck. The antifashion views from Antwerp are a valuable part of our world dialogue on fashion and are unique to that place.

Rome makes its fashion voice heard as Italy's center for haute couture and boutique shopping. The houses of Valentino and Fendi were established in Rome, and the city views itself as connected more to Paris than to Milan's prêt-à-porter. Las Vegas is a city known primarily for entertainment and casinos, with constant media exposure. The local retail venues are the main fashion focus, with destination shopping at the Fashion Show mall and luxury shopping for those who have been successful at the casinos. A fashion week was held there for the first time in 2009. Berlin was an avant-garde fashion city during the early twentieth century and is regaining its position as an artsy, cosmopolitan city. Since the fall of the Berlin Wall, young designers have begun to flourish with the energy of the city and the support of the community. High-end retailers, international boutiques, and local designers have established themselves in a very vibrant, international economy. Berlin's first fashion week was held in 2007. Other top twenty cities in the *Global Language Monitor*'s report ("Top Fashion Cities," 2008) include Hong Kong, Dubai, Singapore, Madrid, Moscow, Santiago, and Stockholm.

The diversity of the global marketplace and the connection between the place and the product hold great appeal. Designers reflect the city in which they work but also bring their own cultural traditions and experiences to their garments. Designers from around the world show in a variety of international fashion weeks in an effort to expand their markets. Though they bring their own style to the event, many of the international attendees are unaware of a designer's nationality. *Women's Wear Daily* staff members (April 4, 2008) suggest that nationality in fashion will cease and become unimportant as global brands direct a uniform message to the market. However, there is a growing desire for individuality that cannot be addressed when the same brand and retail outlets are available in multiple cities around the world. When a fashion product is too accessible, it loses its status and appeal. Individuality is best supported by local designers, whether they work in fashion centers or in cities far-removed. Place provides a richness and multiplicity to our ideas so that it deserves to be nurtured. Thus, fashion centers around the world facilitate global markets for fashion while designers take advantage of their unique position in time and place.

FASHION FOCUS FROM THE FIELD: CULTURAL DRESS FOR SOMALI IMMIGRANTS

As immigrants adapt to a new home, dress can become an important issue. There is debate in the Somali community over what is traditional, what is appropriate to wear on a daily basis, and the need to wear Islamic dress, as well as real concern about losing their traditional culture. Islamic dress is easy to purchase or make, but the traditional, colorful fabrics of East Africa are more difficult to acquire and can cost ten times their original price. This applies especially to the most fashionable and prestigious fabrics, as popular colors change by the season. Many Somalis have reserved these fabrics for special events like weddings. The fabrics are primarily sourced from India, Japan, South Korea, Kenya, or Tanzania. When Somalis first came to the United States as refugees with very few possessions, the only way to get these fabrics was for someone to hand carry them back from East Africa, making them both rare and expensive. However, within the last decade some manufacturers have started to reach the Somali diaspora market directly. Interest in these textiles on the part of non-Somalis is limited because garments are not sold ready-to-wear and must be sewn at home or by a tailor. In addition, the fabric is not considered an art form, thus is not particularly attractive to collectors. Somali men tend to wear Western dress, a trend that started before they immigrated.

Summary

- Traditional fashion centers require financial and cultural resources, manufacturing capabilities, a large, inexpensive labor force, and centers for shopping.
- Modern fashion centers are focused on cultural commodities that support the symbolic production and consumption of fashion.
- A polycentric view of global fashion places value on the unique qualities of person and place reflected in apparel.
- A thriving fashion community is an indicator of a city's position in the world.
- The top five fashion centers—London, Milan, New York, Paris, and Tokyo—have distinct identities but face global competition from emerging fashion cities that present original views on fashion to the world consumer.
- Emerging fashion centers face challenges in technology, industry infrastructure, and business expertise. Leadership and direction are often fragmented, and design, production, and marketing efforts are unbalanced.
- A successful runway showing in Paris or New York continues to provide validation for many new international designers.
- Strong design schools support and enhance fashion centers, providing training, new talent, and resources.
- Unique retail locations are essential to a strong fashion center.
- Strong cultural resources augment the creative energy of a fashion center.

Vocabulary

- bespoke
- commodity
- global
- indigenous
- polycentric
- street fashion
- UNESCO

Discussion

1. What are the advantages and disadvantages of holding a fashion week event for established or emerging fashion centers?
2. Most major fashion centers are in the northern hemisphere. Are there advantages related to this location?
3. Do you support government involvement in establishing and maintaining a city as a fashion center? Why or why not?
4. What strategies and resources would you suggest for a designer who wants to design locally and market globally?
5. If cities or countries thought about regional partnerships, as suggested by Richard Florida, author of *Who's Your City*, what would be the advantages or disadvantages for the fashion industry?
6. When a designer travels, bringing back inspiration from a new location, how does the designer's own culture act as a filter? Would garments designed locally and marketed internationally be more appealing to the international consumer, or is a cultural filter needed for global success?
7. What impact might technology and virtual reality have on the success and growth of global fashion centers?

7

A LOOK TO THE FUTURE

Fashion has always been about constant change, but with the rapid development of new technologies, fashion is likely to change even more dramatically in the next few decades. Futuristic fashion has long been linked to the image of space: sleek, form-fitting garments with helmets that perform a range of tasks from transportation to transformation. The reality of future fashion is focused on the current and critical needs of our society, including health and safety, sustainability, preservation of the past, and the discovery of meaningful ways to bring beauty and pleasure into our lives. This chapter explores some of the major issues and developments that will influence how designers work and make decisions in the future.

Technology

Changes in fashion are often linked to innovation in textiles. From the development of the first manufactured fiber, researchers have been attempting to mimic nature. Rayon was developed to imitate silk, and spandex improved on the natural properties of rubber. Our technology has now moved us beyond nature, allowing the design of smart textiles with specific properties for a wide range of functional and aesthetic applications. Smart textiles can sense and react to different environments and stimuli using a variety of materials, chemistry, electronics, and nanotechnology. When smart textiles are used as part of a system that works with the wearer's needs, the results can improve comfort, protection, performance, health, and aesthetic appearance. The success of the system depends on technology that is unobtrusive and comfortable so that it will actually be worn, and it must be reliable, particularly for medical and emergency uses. For example, a garment that monitors the vital signs and performance of an athlete must allow for freedom of movement without wires and extra weight. It might also need to wick away moisture, provide UV protection, and be easy to clean. To be viable on the market, the total system needs to be affordable and easy care.

Smart textiles

Some smart textiles incorporate glass, ceramics, metal, or carbon with the fibers, yarn, or a finish to produce the desired functional properties. Passive properties such as selective permeability, wicking, static dissipation, and antimicrobial protection are characteristic of one group of smart textiles. Materials with environmentally responsive properties—for example, phase-change materials that can absorb, store, and release heat while the material changes from solid to liquid and back, or photovoltaic fibers that can collect solar or light energy—dynamically interact with the wearer. Fiber-optic textiles, electroactive polymers, and heating textiles are examples of electronically controllable or sensor/actuator properties that pick up signals from the environment. The environmentally responsive textiles are the most "intelligent" on their own, while the others incorporate the ability to be controlled or changed using an external force. Alternately, a sensor can be attached to a textile or garment to interact with a control unit.

Nanotechnology

Nanotechnology allows materials to be designed from their smallest parts: atoms and molecules. This creates the opportunity to develop textiles that are stronger, lighter, or more conductive or that can change color and shape. This technology has the potential to dramatically change how clothing is perceived. From simple problems with our everyday clothing such as stains, wrinkles, or odor to the development of wireless communication methods for medical, military, and personal uses, nanotechnology has the potential to improve the quality of life and make the environment more sustainable. For example, nanoparticles of silver create antibacterial properties in clothing or can be used to generate color with light reflection rather than dye. Because the size of the particles is so small, they attach to the fibers in a way that maintains the original hand of the fabric while providing better performance and durability. Microencapsulation is a type of nanotechnology that creates small bubbles in the fibers that can hold products including perfume, lotion, medicine, or insect repellents that are released on the wearer's skin and that last through approximately thirty washes.

Wearable technology

Wearable technology integrates clothing and technology, essentially making clothing smart. It goes beyond smart textiles because wearable technology must be designed to fit and interact with the body in the greater environment. Combining hard technology with soft textiles so that neither element is compromised is challenging. First conceived as little more than a computer strapped to the waist, wearable technology is moving toward garments that will allow people to communicate, listen to music, get directions, or be reminded of appointments without wires or using their hands. Through integrated sensors and actuators, clothing can change in response to environmental or social conditions, or the wearer's personal preferences or emotions. Sight- or hearing-impaired individuals could be guided safely and confidently through their day with a garment that could respond to local stimuli. There are a host of health and protection possibilities, from measuring blood sugar to administering light therapy, as well as providing new opportunities for leisure and entertainment. As these technologies develop, it seems promising that even our everyday garments will be more functional.

FASHION FOCUS FROM THE FIELD: LUCY DUNNE: WEARABLE TECHNOLOGY AND PERVASIVE HEALTH CARE

One of the most promising opportunities for the integration of electronic or responsive technologies and clothing is in the area of health care. The vision of so-called pervasive health care is a scenario in which individuals' health and well-being are monitored continuously during everyday activities. Preventative feedback is then supplied to the individual or health-care professional to detect health conditions early and reduce the incidence of emergency care. With current technology, continuous monitoring can be prohibitively invasive and uncomfortable for the patient. The needs for physical comfort and social acceptability become more crucial as the length of time the device must be worn increases. This is where the apparel designer comes in: to develop new monitoring technologies that are comfortable, wearable, and easy to use.

Dr. Lucy Dunne of the University of Minnesota tackles these issues in her wearable technology research. She has a background in apparel design and computer science and hopes to bridge the gap between the fields to integrate their design processes, manufacturing, and markets in an effort to develop this emerging industry. In one project, she developed a shirt that monitors the spinal posture of people who work long hours at a desk or computer. The garment contains a fiber-optic sensor that measures the bend of the spine and uses that information to provide real-time feedback to the user on the computer screen. The device looks and feels like a regular garment and alerts the user only when he or she has been sitting in an unhealthy posture for a period of time.

Aesthetic technology

In addition to its many functional properties, clothing also acts as a primary means of personal and aesthetic expression. Technology can extend the possibilities of expression by creating opportunities that did not exist before and can support new directions in design. Innovations such as the zipper, spandex, and seamless knitting have changed our appearance, but the current innovation directed at the aesthetic

Figure 7.1 Shirt that monitors spinal posture, 2006, courtesy of Lucy Dunne.

qualities of textiles is revolutionary. From digital prints and new yarns to laser cutting and the incorporation of plastics, electronics, and sound, opportunities for creative innovation are endless. Digital printing allows original art to be engineered to fall on the body so that the pattern can be continuous or placed exactly where the designer chooses. Each pattern piece is printed individually, so there is no waste of ink and changes can be made quickly at little cost. Laser cutting can be used to create intricately cut patterns in fabric and leather. This allows many more design options as the labor intensity and cost are dramatically reduced.

Textiles with uniquely beautiful texture or surface and light properties provide inspiration for many designers. Many of these new textiles are reserved for haute couture or very high-end designers due to their limited production and high cost, but this is one of the elements that set them apart from ready-to-wear. New fabrics give rise to new forms, advanced construction and production techniques, and innovative expression.

The technology exists for our clothing to change color, shape, and form while we are wearing it. Our garments can light up or move dynamically, reacting to our environment or personal preferences. Much of the inspiration for new textile technologies is drawn from traditional techniques. The Japanese have been pioneers with innovative advances in textiles. There is national respect for craft traditions that has grounded their scientists and designers as they move the field forward. Reiko Sudo, cofounder of NUNO Textiles, stays true to traditional Japanese handcraft while experimenting with innovative materials to create new textiles. Designer Hussein Chalayan has done considerable experimentation with polymer materials, lights, and electromechanical movement as elements of expression in his work.

Sustainability

Apparel sustainability is not a new concept. Historically, most people owned few garments, as these required valuable resources of both materials and time to make or purchase. Clothing was treated as an investment and was maintained or remade as long as there was useful life left in the textile. By the end of the twentieth century, the Western world had a very different relationship with clothing. Fashion changes regularly with the season and in some cases every few weeks. Currently, ready-to-wear garments are inexpensive and widely available, and consumers can purchase well beyond what they need. Replacing an item because it is worn out is rarely the justification for buying something new. Many Western consumers are caught in a trap of consumerism, feeling that their personal happiness relies on fulfilling a constant need to purchase more, for less money. This pattern of overconsumption cannot be sustained. It has a great negative impact on our environment and on the quality of life for both those involved in the process of making clothing and those consuming fashion.

The countermovement to consumerism and wasteful use of our resources is sustainability. In her 1962 book, *Silent Spring,* Rachel Carson exposed the impact of toxic chemicals on the environment. Sustainability was not and is not a trend. It is a way of living and working that results in "development that meets the needs of the present without compromising the ability of future generations to meet their own needs" (United Nations, 1987). The focus on conscientious production and purchasing has magnified early in the twenty-first century as a result of concerns about global warming, social justice, a worldwide economic crisis, and a growing need to find personal fulfillment.

Much of the apparel industry has been disconnected from these growing concerns. There has been unrealistic pressure on designers, producers, and consumers to make fashion faster and cheaper under a constant demand for new ideas and innovation (Fletcher, 2007), with little regard for the true costs. Though changing perceptions and practices is difficult, it is the very nature of fashion. Motivating the industry and the consumer to adopt more sustainable practices will require two things: (1) Economic value must still be able to be gained from the business, and (2) the products must be desirable. Sustainable fashion will still remain an important part of our world. It helps us communicate, form identities, and fulfill our aesthetic needs. It also provides protection, reflects society, and embraces the diversity in our world.

FASHION FOCUS FROM THE FIELD: NAU

This outdoor clothing company views sustainability as the core of its business plan. Nau makes clothing for men and women that is designed for performance, sustainability, and beauty for wear in the outdoor and urban landscape. Fulfilling all three criteria is challenging, particularly when combined with the company's radical paradigm shift from the traditional apparel business. Nau has designed its products and the entire company based on the idea that businesses must take on a bigger responsibility for what happens in a community than generating a profit. Environmental and human resources benefit from the 2 percent of sales that go to charitable organizations. The company faced some financial challenges due to overly ambitious growth, but it was acquired by Horny Toad, a company with similar values and a commitment to sustainability.

Transparency is one way Nau shares this commitment; thus its information technology and supply chain are set up to follow every detail of production from start to finish. Computer-aided design technology has enabled the company to digitally develop and deliver patterns to its vendor, providing more control regarding style and fit issues. This saves time and costs and reduces the carbon footprint with less paper and fuel for travel. Nau has also helped to develop over 300 fabrics that are sustainable, designed for performance, and beautiful. The company has consciously chosen to produce its garments in locations that are close to its material suppliers and have the necessary technical expertise, including Canada, China, Thailand, and Turkey. A third party is used to review compliance with their standards.

Slow fashion is a countertrend to the unsustainable nature of fast fashion and the exhaustion of constantly pursuing the next trend. Slow fashion embraces knowing where materials are sourced and how they are made; knowing that workers are fairly paid and protected from human rights violations; knowing that the clothing is of high quality; and knowing that the care and disposal of the garment are environmentally friendly (Fletcher, 2008). A new model is emerging in which our focus shifts from wasteful, privileged overabundance to embrace a more equitable, shared responsibility for the earth's resources. Translated into fashion, it means quality over quantity. Much depends on changing attitudes and reducing the appeal of consumerism. This would be a dramatic shift in how we think about fashion, shopping, and caring for and discarding our clothing. However, new opportunities for innovation will be created that will move fashion in a new direction.

The complexity of creating a more sustainable apparel industry reaches across all elements of the business, from production to retail to the consumer. Solutions will emerge that require support and adaptability, particularly from company leaders and entrepreneurs who can envision the long-term value of investments. All businesses can become more sustainable by reducing, reusing, and recycling their resources; however, there are specific decisions that a designer can make to support a more sustainable future for fashion.

Environment

Fashion's impact on the environment has received the most attention with regard to the development of more sustainable fiber-producing practices. Resources, including land and labor, are limited. Ultimately, fiber usage needs to be reduced, despite increasing demand. There is no clear choice between growing natural fibers and making synthetic fibers with regard to their impact on the environment. The entire process of production as well as the life cycle of the garment contributes to making an environmentally friendly decision. Natural fibers, often preferred by higher-end designers, are frequently thought to be a more sustainable choice because they are renewable and biodegradable. However, the use of chemical fertilizers and pesticides along with high land and water usage can make cotton a poor choice. Organic cotton is highly desired but cannot be produced in the quantities needed to meet demand. Flax, wool, and silk place fewer demands on the environment than cotton but require more labor-intensive processing. With improved finishing technology, hemp, ramie, and jute are being reconsidered for apparel, particularly for use in blends with cotton, linen, or synthetics. These fibers are both environmentally friendly and low cost.

The quality of synthetic fibers has improved since researchers have learned more about how to engineer fibers with different properties. They are lower in cost to purchase and maintain but are often viewed as less desirable than natural fibers even though they are produced with less toxic impact. The petroleum used to make nylon, polyester, acrylic, olefin, and spandex is shrinking in supply, so there are multiple reasons to develop new fiber sources that are renewable and nontoxic. Bamboo, corn, and soy are being developed as renewable resources for use as raw materials for new synthetic fibers. However, caution must be exercised, as many cellulose-based fibers are still processed with chemicals, negating any perceived environmental benefit. Recycling fiber is another method to reduce the impact on the environment. For example, Capilene polyester can be recycled to renew itself using 70 percent less energy than production of new polyester, a program developed by Teijin Mill in Japan and Patagonia in the United States. Patagonia was also the first to use polyester made from recycled PET soda bottles, which has resulted in less dependence on oil and the reduction of landfill waste and air, water, and soil pollution.

The processes of adding color to and finishing a textile have long been a concern with respect to the environment. These processes account for the second-highest use of water and energy behind fiber production. Newer methods of dyeing and finishing that use less water and energy are being utilized, and new processes continue to be developed. In addition to being more environmentally friendly, these new methods are less expensive, so they support a long-term commitment to more sustainable practices.

Measuring the carbon footprint of a company is one way to evaluate the environmental impact of different practices. A carbon footprint measures the amount of carbon dioxide (CO_2), which can contribute to global warming, that is produced by a person, company, or product. As consumers demand more information about the products they buy, an objective rating system is needed. The Carbon Trust in the United Kingdom helps companies to reduce emissions from their supply chains by investing in low-carbon products and services. They also have a certification program that allows companies to label the carbon footprint of a product. The CarbonFree Certified product label allows companies to identify their products as being climate neutral based on an annual analysis of production, shipping, operations, and disposal. Many other countries are working to develop similar certification and labeling programs.

FASHION FOCUS FROM THE FIELD: MARKS AND SPENCER PLAN A

The popular U.K. retailer Marks and Spencer (M&S) has been in the business of selling clothing, home products, and groceries for over 100 years. M&S launched Plan A (there is no Plan B) in January 2007 as a map for sustainability across the company that would result in carbon neutrality by 2012. The company, its supply chain, and its customers are all involved with the help of external partners, including the Carbon Trust. The goal is to become carbon neutral and send no waste to landfills; increase sustainable sourcing; set high standards in ethical trading; and help customers and employees live a healthier lifestyle. Most of the plan's 100 points are not difficult to follow; they just require changing habits.

One project is to donate used clothing to the Oxfam Clothes Exchange, thus raising money to support those in poverty as well as keeping tons of clothing out of landfills. Reducing packaging helps as well, and when M&S began to charge for shopping bags, usage dropped by 80 percent. Sourcing fair trade products, reducing and composting food waste, and using only cruelty-free testing on cosmetics and household products are other examples of the diverse areas that are part of Plan A. In May 2008, M&S partnered with its supplier, MAS, and opened its first eco-factory in Sri Lanka to manufacture lingerie. The company was awarded the World Environment Gold Medal for International Corporate Achievement in Sustainable Development in 2007 for its exemplary model.

Process

Designers have the responsibility for selecting fabrics with fibers and finishes that come from easily renewable resources, have the minimum impact on the environment, and also have the desired aesthetic and performance qualities (Baugh,

2008). Designing a garment that reduces the environmental impact is a challenging and complex task. Part of the challenge will be to create a profit from fewer, well-designed pieces that offer meaning, purpose, and value to the consumer. Design decisions influence pattern shapes and fabric utilization and can have a large impact on the amount of scrap fabric that is generated during cutting. Current waste from cutting is estimated at 10 to 20 percent. By combining design sketching with patternmaking in a more direct way, shapes can be created that fit more compactly on the fabric, with less waste. Starting with the fabric rather than a sketch may be one way to inspire innovative pattern shapes (Rissanen, 2009). Garments that are wrapped and draped, or created from basic geometric shapes, are related to historical and cultural practices that support the conservation of resources. Knitting a garment in which one forms the individual shapes needed creates no waste in comparison with a cut-and-sewn garment from either knit or woven fabric (Rissanen, 2009). Minimal seam allowances are common in mass-produced garments because they reduce costs and streamline production sewing. However, more generous seam allowances and hems may allow for a greater range of alterations as an individual's body changes or a garment is fitted to a second owner: ultimately a choice that can conserve economic and environmental resources.

Developing a design in which all the components can be recycled or are made from recycled materials is an environmentally friendly decision. For example, Patagonia's Eco Shell performance jacket is made from recycled polyester and can be fully recycled through the Common Threads Garment Recycling Program. Nike Grind is a program that recycles used athletic shoes of any brand into surfaces for sports and playgrounds. Locally, many design entrepreneurs recycle materials from discarded garments to make newly designed apparel. Selecting buttons made from vegetable ivory derived from the tagua nut instead of plastic is another environmentally friendly choice. Thoughtful consideration about final care requirements to avoid unnecessary dry-cleaning and selection of packaging, labels, and hangtags that are environmentally friendly can reinforce a company's commitment to sustainability.

Offshore production has been common practice for domestic manufacturers because labor costs have been substantially more competitive. In response to concerns about the impact of transportation on the environment, there is growing interest in producing products closer to the point of sale, moving textile and apparel production facilities into closer proximity, or reviving vertical manufacturing. This may be very challenging as there are few domestic factories, few individuals with the expertise to manage them, and a small, untrained labor force. Oceanic Sportswear, a manufacturer in British Columbia, divides its production between domestic and offshore factories. There is less direct profit from the domestic production, but its customers value the domestic production, and the company believes that it gives them an advantage with customer service (Dunn, 2008). Louis Vuitton consciously transports goods by boat or rail, which is 40 percent less polluting than by air. As international labor and trade costs continue to rise, some forms of domestic production may hold greater appeal for apparel manufacturers.

More industry organizations are combining efforts to support industry-wide goals to conserve environmental resources. In Hong Kong, the Sustainable Fashion Business Consortium has made a commitment to recycling fabric and reducing energy consumption by 20 percent, and they are working with the World Wide Fund to start a low-carbon measuring program for the industry. The Nordic Fashion Association plans to develop a ten-year code of conduct plan, the Nordic Initiative Clean and Ethical project (NICE), to address a range of environmental and social issues. The No Dirty Gold campaign asks retailers and consumers not to purchase jewelry made with gold that has been mined without regard for protecting the safety of the environment and the workers from toxic chemicals or explosions. Many jewelers are now using reclaimed gold that has been returned to a twenty-four-karat standard and support the use of "conflict-free" gems, those that are mined responsibly and are not sold to fund war (Lennon, 2009). In the future, additional support will come from more new graduates who will join the apparel industry from programs with a focus on sustainability, including the University of Delaware, Chelsea College of Art and Design, California College of the Arts, Centre for Sustainable Fashion at the London College of Fashion, and Royal Melbourne Institute of Technology.

Human resources

Human resources are the most valuable asset of a society or a business. Thus the life, liberty, and security of an individual are not only rights but also responsibilities regardless of the person's role as an employee, employer, consumer, or government official. The history of labor in the apparel industry illustrates the efforts made to protect workers in industrialized countries. Issues of health and safety, working hours, child labor, and compensation have been of concern since the start of the Industrial Revolution and the era of mass production. Global problems with human rights and the work environment continue. Standards are difficult to enforce due to the remote location of many of the factories and lack of commitment from local owners. Different cultures may view workers as a commodity rather than a valuable resource, and increasing profits continues to be the main concern.

In the past, the apparel industry has mainly focused on achieving the best price, the best quality, and the shortest lead time for its products in order to stay competitive. Most apparel companies have their fabrics and garments produced by factories that are contracted to cut and sew. Global sourcing and offshore production have been a way to operate that made strong economic sense. However, awareness of human rights violations by many apparel companies that made products in countries with emerging economies exploded in the press in the late twentieth century. Stories about sweatshop labor including never-ending workweeks, substandard pay and no overtime pay, no safety measures, and child labor were common. Reports described workers who, often poor and uneducated, were harassed, cheated, and denied basic work rights. Work conditions can be negatively impacted due to price competition, inefficiency and greed, pressure from the purchasing company for last-minute changes, unreasonable price demands, and unrealistic delivery schedules. Decisions and policies made domestically can have huge consequences for global vendors, often without just cause. For example, one vendor was under a competitive bid, with the lowest price driven to the point where there was negligible margin for any profit. Thus a difficult decision needed to be made: agree to the lowest price that barely covered expenses and risk the stability of the factory or reject the bid and put the factory in certain danger of losing work that would at least keep it operational.

The history of consumer rights and protection is more recent. The first Consumer Bill of Rights was signed into law by U.S. President Kennedy in 1962, and an expanded version was adopted by the United Nations in 1985. The consumer has the rights to choice, to safety, to information, to a voice, to redress or remedy, to environmental health, to service, and to consumer education. Recently there has been a shift toward a more ethical consumer whose concern has expanded beyond his or her individual needs to support global issues. Consumers are asking who made their clothes, where they were made, and how they were made, and they are holding companies and designers accountable.

Companies have begun to develop ethical sourcing programs within a movement toward corporate social responsibility. This means that the company takes responsibility for the effect of its activities and decisions on consumers, employees, communities, and the environment. The level of commitment varies, but most now have public statements and policies regarding their standards and means of inspecting and resolving human rights issues for all those in their supply chain. Improving conditions in the factories with safety standards, legal working hours, and fair wages has gained importance. Transparency regarding environmental practices has also improved. Unfortunately, standards and inspections by the company or an independent agency have not ensured consistent advances; thus work supporting human rights and the environment remains to be done, both locally and globally.

Addressing consumer concerns has become an important strategy for apparel companies to maintain their market share. However, criteria for decisions, currently often based solely on price, quality, and speed to market, will need to be expanded to include business requirements, quality assurance, social responsibility, and sustainability. Consumers are savvy and will be looking at the core values and practices of apparel companies rather than simply responding to superficial market claims.

Apparel companies also have a responsibility to their direct employees; however, building and maintaining a strong, innovative, and dedicated team of employees have not been a big concern. The traditional system of master/apprentice training, high competition, low wages and benefits, and little job security, as well as a common practice of frequent job changes, is shifting. Smaller, entrepreneurial companies still make up the largest percentage of the industry, but the growth of huge corporations created through mergers and buyouts now dominates the market. Pressures to stay competitive on brand image, price, and speed to market exist at both ends of the spectrum. When these pressures are combined with concerns about the environment and the economy, stress levels can escalate. On the corporate side, burnout is common, particularly among midcareer designers. Too many hours spent working at a computer in a cubical, attending meetings, traveling, and working overtime can deflate an individual's energy and creativity. Owning a small business has its own set of challenges, primarily concerning time and money, that can diminish an individual's ability to thrive.

As the industry shifts to a more environmentally friendly model of business, finding ways to sustain the innovative energy of the individuals involved also deserves attention. Investments that support a more equitable work/life balance are likely to improve the quality of both life and work for individuals and businesses. It will be critical for designers to take a leadership role in the process. The change will be over the long term; choices will be difficult and transparency essential. Consumers expect more than great aesthetics, good quality, and value; they want to feel good about supporting a viable, thriving company that practices environmental and social sustainability.

Maintaining craft traditions

With the increased focus on sustainability, there is interest in looking back to more traditional methods of production and consumption for examples of things that worked well in the past. When mass-produced garments became readily available in the market, many considered it a luxury to be able to purchase clothing from a store or catalog. An embarrassing stigma came to be attached to garments that were handmade or homemade, indicating that you lacked the resources to purchase clothing ready-made. The status of high-quality custom sewing and haute couture was unknown or forgotten by many, as the compliment to a well-constructed handmade garment became, "It looks just like store bought!" While the quality of ready-to-wear apparel is generally very good, the perception of handmade products is reversing. Embracing the skills of a designer who respects the materials and the process of making is of increasing value to many people. Clothing that is thoughtful, sustainable, and beautiful is becoming the luxury of the twenty-first century.

Alabama Chanin is a company that crafts limited-edition apparel with special attention to slow design and environmentally friendly practices. The garments are made from a combination of organic and recycled materials and constructed entirely by hand. Local artisans from a small community in Alabama work in their homes to produce the pieces. The artisans are owners of their own businesses, purchasing raw materials from the Alabama Chanin facility, setting their own prices, and then selling them back to Alabama Chanin. The company has been quite successful in creating a market for its elegant garments that are touched by the hand and the heart. Its business model has been sustainable since the first project in 2000, and it continues to help preserve American craft traditions and community-based culture. Natalie Chanin, owner, has also been active in giving workshops to share her techniques. This is a unique example in a culture that is being led by technology and driven by design but is starved of imagination (Naisbit, 2006).

Crafts and craft traditions are part of the material culture records of our society, though recent generations have had little interest in learning those skills. However, the current popularity of high-touch experiences based on craft traditions, including do-it-yourself projects, knitting, scrapbooking, or dance, is evidence of a growing countertrend. High-tech lifestyles in our society have left a void in our lives. The speed, instant response, and reduced face-to-face contact with coworkers, friends, and family can create the feeling of being overwhelmed, disconnected, and impatient. Slowing down, making personal connections, and using your hands may provide some balance to our technology-focused lives as well as support innovative

Figure 7.2. Top created during Alabama Chanin workshop, 2007, courtesy of E. Bye.

thinking connected to the act of making something (Wagner, 2008). A unique kind of thinking goes on during a hands-on activity that supports creative and critical thinking. Collaborations between craft, technology, and design can create a synergy between traditional craft processes and industrial methods that may lead to innovation. For example, textile designer Lesley Sealey and fashion designer Roger Lee of i.e. uniform blend a traditional craft such as embroidery with a nontraditional fabric like a laminate to develop a new aesthetic. Knitwear designers often experiment with a pattern by hand before transferring it to a knitting machine.

Globally, there are other examples of the value of maintaining craft traditions. Hand embroidery in India is greatly valued and has become a distinctive element of modern Indian fashion design. The knitting traditions of Scandinavia and Ireland required few tools, were a source of income for many who lived in rural areas, and were valued for their individual characteristics that distinguish them from mass-

Figure 7.3 Thimble dress by Ashley Wokasch of Calpernia Peach, screen-printed cotton, 2009, courtesy of the designer, photographer Ryan Cloutier.

produced sweaters. The current generation of new knitters has a strong interest in exploring these knitting traditions. Kyoto, Japan, had a strong tradition of excellent weaving that has transferred to modern textile production. Quilt making continues to be a popular craft tradition in the United States, following values of sustainability related to thrift, precision, hard work, and beauty.

Craft traditions from Africa have been embraced to address the International Trade Center's Millennium Development goals to reduce poverty and improve environmental conditions with the use of recycled and organic materials. Supportive companies from the international fashion community have worked with small communities to develop projects and small businesses to make jewelry, crocheted bags, sweaters, and other garments for export. Creating jobs that rely on craft traditions brings a unique product to the market and hope to many who have been impacted by war, disease, and drought. With production being up to four times more costly in Africa than in Asia, the center's motivation to help build a secure economic foundation for the community is stronger than the need for large profits (Hume, 2009).

Consumers may be motivated to support companies that embrace craft traditions because they offer a more genuine connection to the maker and the materials than a mass-produced garment. The desire to invest in a unique, one-of-a-kind garment touched by the imperfections of the human hand is a response to the consumerism that has developed. Maintaining craft traditions also plays a historical and future role in supporting innovation and creative thinking in conjunction with new technologies.

Improved fit

Finding garments that fit well is a challenge for many consumers, and improving fit is part of improving the quality of apparel. The return of merchandise due to improper size or poor fit is a costly problem for retailers and consumers. When consumers have difficulty finding something to fit from racks of ready-to-wear, they often feel that there is something wrong with their body. Nothing is wrong with individual bodies! Problems originate from the sizing systems that most manufacturers use. When consumers are able to purchase a garment that fits well and makes them feel good, they are likely to wear that garment longer and be satisfied with fewer garments. Shopping for a pair of jeans that fit well is an ongoing quest for many women and often results in many pairs of purchased but unworn jeans in the closet. They are unworn because they do not fit well, putting unnecessary strain on personal and environmental resources.

Measuring the human body is critical to developing garments to fit the body, and many techniques have been developed. Historically, most people wore garments that were custom fit by an experienced professional or fitted and sewn at home, while today the garments we wear are mass produced and sized. During this transition, we lost the ability to recognize good fit and the expertise to make custom-fitted apparel. All bodies are unique, and expecting everyone to wear standardized clothing rather than developing clothing to fit each individual is a practice that needs to change. Measuring the body and applying the measurements to a pattern are essential steps to improving garment fit.

FASHION FOCUS FROM THE FIELD: LIZ CLAIBORNE—PARTNERSHIP WITH CORNELL UNIVERSITY

Designers and patternmakers usually see the garments they are developing only on the company fit model or a dress form. Through a partnership with researchers at Cornell University, patternmakers at Liz Claiborne were able to see how one style of pants looked on more than 200 women of all sizes and shapes. Body scans were taken of women in a scan leotard and wearing the best-fitting pants from the range of sizes provided by the company. These women had the same demographics as Liz Claiborne customers.

Researchers were able to compare the two scans to determine the fit at multiple body locations such as the waist, hip, or inseam. They discovered that the body proportions in the scanned group were different from those of Liz Claiborne's fit model and their sizing system. With further analysis, the researchers were able to make recommendations to improve the sizing system. When the patternmakers reviewed side-by-side images of the women in the scan suit and wearing the pants, they were amazed. The experience provided better insight into how standard sizes actually fit different body types. They also had a better understanding of the range of shapes that wear a single size. The goal of the researchers is to develop a tool that can be used by apparel companies to improve the fit of their garments.

A body scanner is a noncontact instrument for obtaining body measurements that can also provide a permanent record for future reference. The scanner uses a white light or laser to capture a 360-degree image of the body in less than fifteen seconds, and it can generate a variety of reliable measurements. International efforts have begun to scan representative populations from different countries so that accurate, up-to-date sizing systems can be designed. The 2001 SizeUK project scanned 11,000 men and women, followed by SizeUSA and SizeKorea. Thailand, Mexico, China, Brazil, and Australia have plans for similar projects. Analysis of the data will be used to develop sizing systems that more accurately meet the needs of a variety of consumers.

The concept of mass customization provides a model for designing and making custom-fitted garments for the individual (see chapter 3). Some companies have developed the technology to use scan data from an individual to generate a custom pattern. However, considerable research and development are required before this technology will be widely available. Issues that increase the complexity of consumer

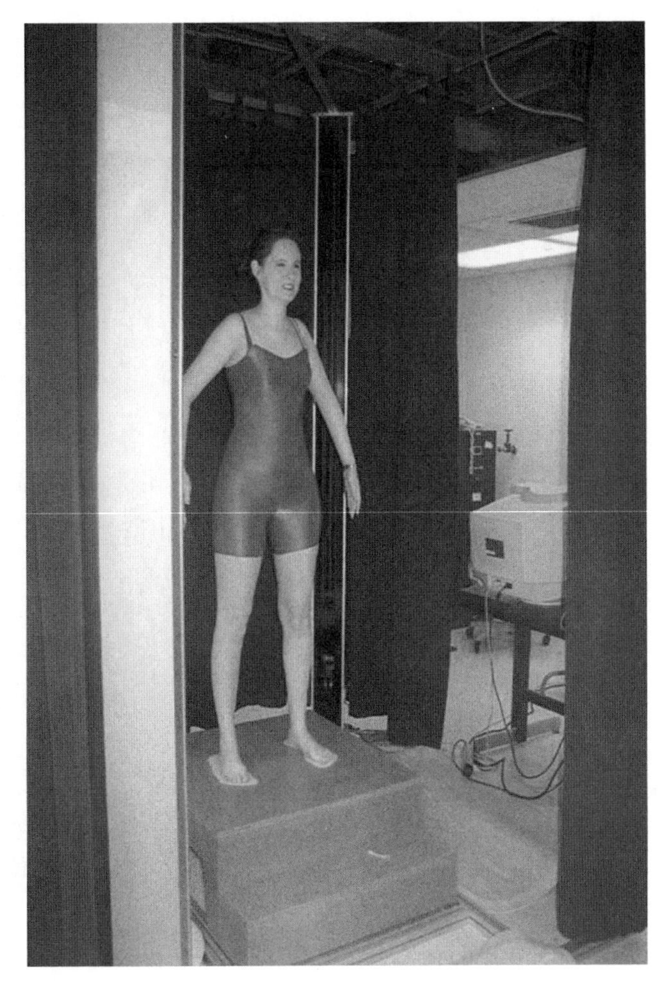

Figure 7.4 Participant ready to be scanned in a Human Solutions body scanner, courtesy of the Human Dimensioning© Lab at the University of Minnesota.

satisfaction with fit include comfort and ease preferences, and variables such as garment design and fabric variations. Consider the difference in how people prefer the fit of a tailored wool suit, a pair of jeans, or a swimsuit.

Though the original goal of body-scanning technology was to use measurements to create custom patterns and garments, the scan image can be modified to act as a personal avatar. This creates opportunities for virtual try-on, size prediction, and personal shopper applications (Loker, Ashdown, Cowie, & Schoenfelder, 2004) that can help consumers shop for clothing using nontraditional practices that may result in improved satisfaction. For example, in a partnership with Alvanon, customers at Levi's can be scanned and given recommendations for jeans that will best fit their body type (Beckett, 2008). In addition, Levi's collects valuable information regarding differences in body type that can help with future sizing and merchandising issues.

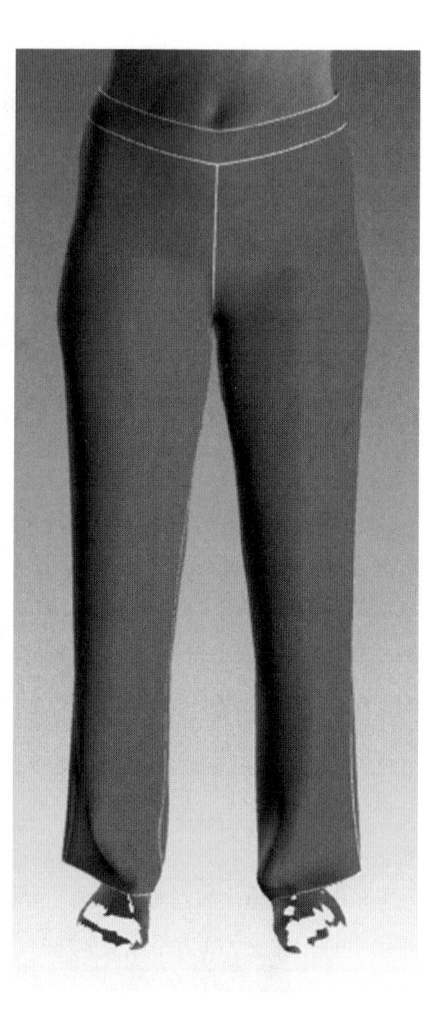

Figure 7.5 Virtual fit model developed using Optitex 3-D software, 2009, courtesy of the Human Dimensioning© Lab at the University of Minnesota.

The next frontier in collecting and analyzing body data for application to apparel may be dynamic anthropometry, or measuring the body in motion. Garments are traditionally fit with the body in a static standing pose, and the model may sometimes be asked to sit, stretch, or bend. In reality, our bodies move and bend in a variety of positions, constantly changing shape, length, and width. Motion-capture systems create a digital record of the body in motion using sensors that are attached to the body or the garment. Understanding how this range of measurements and shapes affects fit and design has the potential to improve the functionality of performance and protective apparel as well as everyday garments.

Luxury design

Luxury: an over-the-top, sumptuous, beyond-the-necessary, indulgent product, service, or attitude that creates a feeling of pleasure. Though most often associated with the lavish and expensive, pleasure also can be generated by things that are simple and inexpensive. No doubt expensive jewelry, designer clothes, and vacation homes are luxuries, but sleeping late and cream in your coffee are luxuries as well. Veblen's theory of conspicuous consumption suggests that many people acquire luxury products or services to publicly display their wealth, thus increasing their social status. Historically, royalty and aristocratic society displayed their wealth and set themselves apart from common people in all aspects of their dress, material possessions, and lifestyle. With the rise of the middle class, more people aspired to rise to the next social level; thus there was an almost constant adoption of new fashion and practices by the upper levels of society in their effort to maintain their status of distinction. Owning the latest limited-edition "It" handbag and employing a personal chef are current examples. These behaviors are the foundation of consumerism, though the details have changed over time.

Luxury designer fashion started with Charles Frederick Worth, and following his model, the early members of the haute couture dressed the aristocracy, celebrities, and the wealthy. Exquisite fabrics, lavish embellishments, parties, and exceptional personal service were the mode. Following World War I, luxury fashion was more informal, simplified, and less extravagant; casual dress became the standard for leisure activities. Coco Chanel understood this change and, by adapting her designs, thrived under the new definition of luxury. Her unstructured knit sportswear adorned with costume jewelry appealed to many women. Paris haute couture remained the center of luxury fashion until the youth movement of the 1960s shifted the focus to the emerging social issues of equality, social responsibility, and mother earth. Yves Saint Laurent adapted his business by adopting the first nonluxury fabric to be used in haute couture: denim.

A brand is molded to strategically differentiate the unique design, material, craftsmanship, and performance of its image and products. It is a guarantee of exclusivity that holds a unique position in the market, elevating desire and commanding premium pricing (Okonkwo, 2007). Branding emerged as a valuable commodity in the 1980s as businesses were merged, acquired, and aligned into an accumulation of power (Okonkwo, 2007). Bernard Arnault became president of Moët Hennessy - Louis Vuitton (LVMH) in 1989, creating the world's largest conglomerate of luxury goods. With over sixty companies under this umbrella, Arnault is now chairman and CEO of this influential company. The demand for luxury goods exploded in the 1990s as brands grew in their power to influence consumers.

Many consumers who aspire to own luxury goods will be purposely frugal when buying basic products so that they can afford to purchase the more visible luxury products that they desire. In China, Levi's is positioned as a luxury product. Though it can take up to six months to save for an entry-level premium pair of jeans, the higher-cost premium jeans are in more demand. For many Chinese, it is worth the extra month of saving to purchase the higher-status jeans (Beckett, 2008). Some consumers are not interested in the authenticity of luxury goods and are satisfied with purchasing products that resemble, or have "the look" of, the

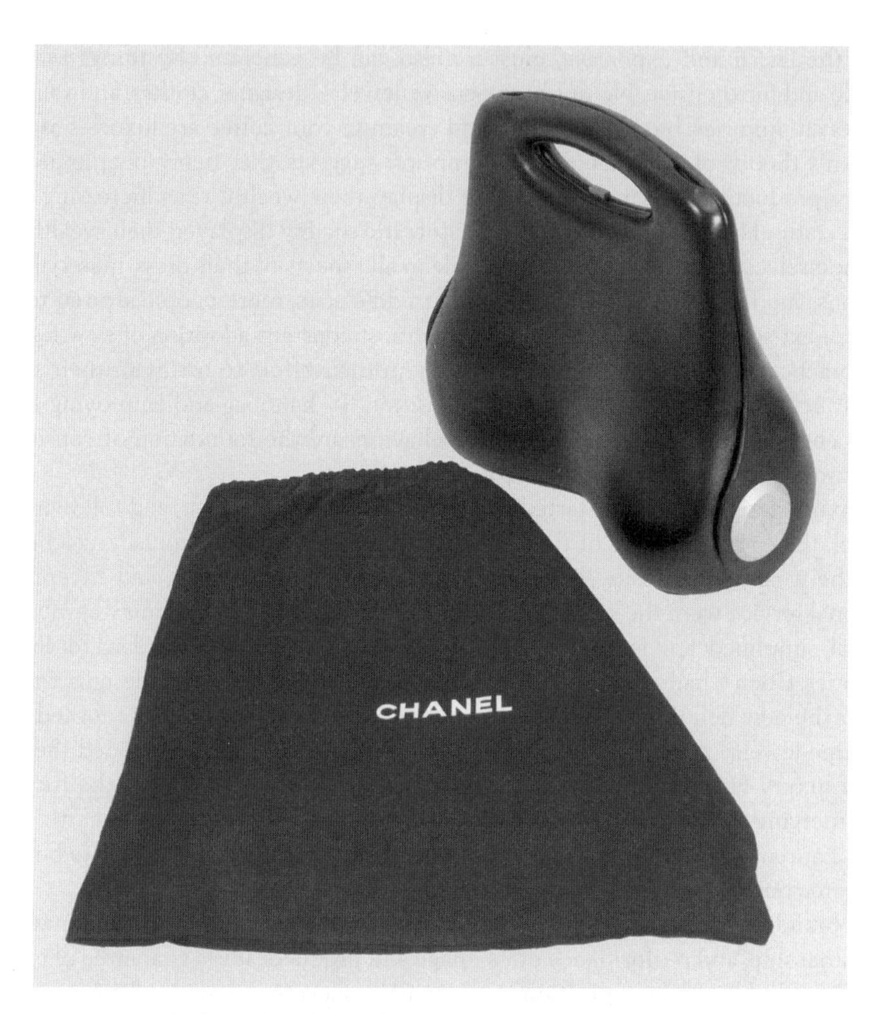

Figure 7.6 Limited-edition Chanel 2005 handbag and black dust bag, polyethylene, leather, metal, 1998, courtesy of the Goldstein Museum of Design, gift of Margot Siegel.

luxury product—preferably an inspiration and not a counterfeit. Consumers can also obtain luxury goods by renting the item to use for a limited time or purchasing pieces secondhand. Though tuxedos are commonly rented, bridal gowns and special-occasion dresses are now offered for loan. Designer handbags can be rented and then exchanged for another the following month.

Some companies are finding it difficult to define their luxury customer: Traditional luxury customers still want established brands such as Hermes and Gucci; however, the new luxury consumers have an increasing desire for unique, one-of-a-kind products that will define them as individuals. With luxury brands becoming more accessible, some brands have started to develop limited editions to offer their customers another level of exclusivity; however, consumers are becoming less dependent on brand names and more confident in their own self-image. There is little interest in wearing a single designer head to toe, and mixing luxury pieces with lower-priced pieces is considered modern. First lady Michelle Obama has received praise from the fashion press and consumers for mixing high-end, mass-market, and local designers in her wardrobe. Consumers have taken responsibility for distinction and originality in their dress partly because designers have failed to do so.

The uniformity and blandness of much of the clothing on the market have extinguished the desire for new clothing (Karimzadeh, 2008). As a result, retailers are forced to compete on price when items cannot be differentiated. The consumer keeps buying inexpensive clothing without any real satisfaction, resulting in a situation that does not serve the retailer or the consumer. U.S. consumers are often proud of their bargains, in contrast to European consumers, who feel they have won when they find and purchase the most perfect item. Perhaps this is one reason why

Figure 7.7 Michelle Obama, 2009, Joyce N. Boghosian, White House photographer.

European women have long been envied for their style. Suzy Menkes, fashion editor for the *International Herald Tribune*, believes that fashion will be moving back toward sustainable luxury and away from fast fashion (Socha, 2008). However, the trend toward high-style fashion at a fraction of the cost has been embraced by consumers as a luxury alternative. Fast fashion's use of limited-edition collections and celebrity endorsements mimics the strategies of luxury brands and supports the consumers' desire for individuality. Fashion retailers such as Target, H&M, and Topshop have made designer fashion accessible and affordable. Consumers understand that fast fashion is temporary, because new designs are always available. But the excitement of a new purchase is also temporary, and consumers must also deal with how to dispose of garments that are no longer valued. The apparel industry has an overload of highly marketed, celebrity-endorsed luxury brands and cheap apparel, which points to the need to redefine luxury.

Luxury in the twenty-first century is truly personal and democratic, but it is a false luxury to ignore our responsibility to society. Donna Karan takes the view that it is a luxury to give to others as well as ourselves (Medina, 2008). In the future, consumers are likely to be more conscientious with regard to luxury. In addition to the tangible qualities of a garment, there will be the intangible luxury of supporting a company that shares similar views on social and environmental responsibility. Luxury will also be found in the experience of personal service and customization options. A variety of innovative partnerships and approaches will be needed to support luxury that respects the needs of unique individuals as well as the collective needs of society.

Summary

- Future fashion is focused on the current and critical needs of our society, including health and safety, sustainability, preservation of the past, and the discovery of meaningful ways to bring beauty and pleasure into our lives.
- Smart textiles can be engineered to improve the comfort, protection, performance, health, and aesthetic appearance of our clothing.
- Overconsumption cannot be maintained and negatively impacts our environment and the quality of life for producers and consumers of fashion.
- Slow fashion supports the conscientious design and use of clothing, transparency of manufacturing processes, and ethical treatment of workers.
- Sustainable design decisions must consider the entire life cycle of a garment.
- Consumers are asking who made their clothes, where they were made, and how they were made, and they are holding companies and designers accountable.
- Synergy between craft traditions and technology can lead to innovation.
- Body-scanning technology and mass-customization methods are being developed to improve the fit of apparel for a variety of body types.
- Definitions of luxury have changed over time from extravagant to responsible.

Vocabulary

- carbon footprint
- dynamic anthropometry
- high-tech/high-touch
- luxury
- nanotechnology
- sustainable
- mass customization
- wearable technology

Discussion

1. Explore the adoption process of new technologies.
2. What new technologies are the most promising in terms of health and safety? Consumer appeal?
3. Develop a working definition of sustainability for the apparel industry. What should the top five priorities for the industry be?
4. Review the market and determine how accessible it is for consumers to locate and purchase sustainable apparel products.
5. Compare the advantages and disadvantages of fast fashion and slow fashion.
6. Develop a strategy to design and promote garments that support the concept of quality over quantity for a variety of consumer groups.
7. What are the long-term and short-term arguments for supporting craft traditions?
8. Is correct fit important to the consumer? Justify your response.
9. Discuss the collaborative partnerships that will be necessary for wearable technology to succeed in the market.
10. Explore the role of luxury in the apparel industry: past, present, and future.

CONCLUSION

Success in the apparel industry depends on coordinated team efforts. The designer's role and responsibility are to provide direction and drive change, with the goal of creating innovative, beautiful garments that meet the consumers' needs and help the company achieve its financial goals. Fashion and change are synonymous, creating continuous opportunities to introduce new ideas and practices. So the energy and vision, and the values and commitment, that designers bring to their work are critical. This book has explored the issues and practices that have an impact on designers as they approach future opportunities and challenges.

Designers have the chance to make a difference in the quality of life for both individuals and society. Garments that are beautiful, functional, and developed with consideration of social and environmental issues can bring meaning and pleasure to the wearer. Responsible use of our natural and human resources encourages more equitable stewardship of our world as resources diminish and populations grow. There is no question that, collectively, we need to take action, but the question of "How?" remains. Designers are comfortable working with ideas and concepts of things that do not exist. Imagining the future depends on their ability to collect information, make new connections between ideas, and take the risk necessary to lead in a new direction. The focus needs to shift beyond a naive perception of fashion to one that includes the full life cycle of a garment. The process of production, consumption, and disposal of clothing, overlaid with the needs and values of local and global communities, offers a broader view of the important position of fashion in society.

The basic challenge of maintaining a fashion business is a constant. A solid financial foundation and ethical practices are essential for a company to grow and respond to changing needs. The challenge of developing products and practices that address the subject of social and environmental responsibility is at the forefront of issues that designers must address. One of the most challenging issues in the apparel industry is consumerism. Most of Western society has been on a trajectory of acquiring more and more products, regardless of need. The increasing consumption of goods has been promoted as economically desirable, and the apparel industry has fully supported the concept. During the early twenty-first century, the world economy has faltered, causing many companies to go out of business and many others to reevaluate their direction and purpose. There has also been a growing tendency toward excess and sameness in fashion, with the assumption that the consumer would continue to buy even when there was nothing new or innovative in the market.

There has been an oversupply of products, businesses, and retail outlets that can no longer be supported; thus the consumer has developed a different set of priorities and needs while the market has simultaneously contracted. Value and integrity now hold more appeal for the consumer than the allure of a marketing campaign. Trust and character make a difference to consumers, who are demanding more authentic, individual attention from the companies they support. Emotional connections, improved communication, and respect for diversity and original ideas are priorities. More than ever, a designer's ability to interpret the needs of customers into focused, innovative concepts and garments will be essential to success and survival.

However, companies and individuals want to do more than survive: They want to thrive. Designers need to establish a clear purpose for their team and model the motivation and energy needed to be forward thinking and acting. Awareness of regional and global trends and broad, reaching changes in our world influence design decisions. Identifying major shifts and translating them early into products, practices, and services that meet the needs of consumers are critical to positioning the product and company to succeed. Some opportunities for the apparel industry exist in the growing concern about health and safety; competition for resources; the growth of China, India, and Africa; the shift back to urban centers; and increasing life expectancy.

Fashion has always been an exciting, dynamic field. Change and competition are rooted in the business, craft, and tradition of the industry and will continue to be part of the future. After the death of Yves Saint Laurent, there was much discussion about who would be the next fashion genius. While a few fashion designers may aspire to that title, most designers have a genuine commitment to the craft regardless of the fame they might achieve. In an article by Guy Trebay (2008), he highlights two quotations that illustrate the importance and seriousness of a designer's responsibility. Artist and film director Jean Renior shares that "The cult of great ideas is dangerous and may destroy the real basis for great achievements, that is the daily, humble work within the framework of a profession" (p. 2). Julie Gilhart, fashion director at Barney's, suggests that it is rare for an individual to be a great designer as well as a celebrity, and the industry may be "closing out a lot of opportunities for people who are original and good and who actually have something to say" (p. 2). There must be an increase in the substance of fashion that goes beyond the hype. Bright, creative designers can invent an innovative twenty-first-century fashion paradigm if they find a balance between their talents and aspirations and the new needs of society. There is a great deal at stake for those who want to compete and thrive.

BIBLIOGRAPHY

Agins, T. (2000). *The end of fashion: How marketing changed the clothing business forever.* New York: Harper Collins.

Ashdown, S. (Ed.) (2007). *Sizing in clothing: Developing effective sizing systems for ready-to-wear clothing.* Cambridge, UK: Woodhead.

Auerbach, J. (1999). *The great exhibition of 1851: A nation on display.* London: Yale University Press.

Azuma, N., & Fernie, J. (2003). Fashion in the globalized world and the role of virtual networks in intrinsic fashion design. *Journal of Fashion Marketing and Management,* 7(4), 413–427.

Baugh, G. (2008). Fibers: Clean and green fiber options. In Hethorn, J., & Ulasewicz, C. (Eds.), *Sustainable fashion: Why now: A conversation about issues, practices and possibilities* (326–357). New York: Fairchild.

Beckett, W. (2008, September 27). Luxury Levi's boom in China. *Women's Wear Daily,* 18.

Benbow-Pfalzgraf, T. (Ed.) (2002). *Contemporary fashion* (2nd ed.). Detroit, MI: St. James Press.

Bhachu, P. (2004). *Dangerous designs: Asian women fashion, the diaspora economies.* London: Routledge.

Bierhals, C. (Ed.) (2007). *Young European fashion designers.* Cologne, Germany: Daab.

Bonacich, E., & Appelbaum, R. P. (2000). *Behind the label: Inequality in the Los Angeles apparel industry.* Berkeley: University of California Press.

Bonsiepe, G. (2007). The uneasy relationship between design and design research. In Michel, R. (Ed.), *Design research now* (25–40). Basel, Switzerland: Birkhäuser.

Braddock Clarke, S. E., & O'Mahony, M. (2006). *Techno textiles 2: Revolutionary fabrics for fashion and design.* London: Thames & Hudson.

Breward, C. (2003). *Fashion.* Oxford: Oxford University Press.

Breward, C. (2004). *Fashioning London: Clothing and the modern metropolis.* Oxford: Berg.

Breward, C., & Gilbert, D. (Eds.) (2006). *Fashion's world cities.* Oxford: Berg.

Brousson, J. (1925). *Anatole France himself: A Boswellian record.* Philadelphia: J. B. Lippincott.

Burns, L., & Bryant, N. (2002). *Business of fashion.* New York: Fairchild.

Chan, D. (Ed.) (2008). *Young Asian fashion designers.* Cologne, Germany: Daab.

Conti, S. (2008, November 12). Fashion's new circuit: Social networks. *Women's Wear Daily,* 9.

Craik, J. (1994). *The face of fashion: Cultural studies in fashion.* London: Routledge.

da Cruz, E. (2004, October). Miyake, Kawakubo, and Yamamoto: Japanese fashion in the twentieth century. *Heilbrunn timeline of art history, Metropolitan Museum of Art.* Retrieved February 15, 2009, from http://www.metmuseum.org/toah/hd/jafa/hd_jafa.htm.

d'Astous, A., & Saint-Louis, O. (2005). National versus store brand effects on consumer evaluation of a garment. *Journal of Fashion Marketing and Management,* 9(3), 306–317.

Dickson, M. A., & Eckman, M. (2006). Social responsibility: The concept as defined by apparel and textile scholars. *Clothing and Textiles Research Journal,* 24(3), 178–191.

Dunn, B. (2008, March 18). Proximity pays for Canadian manufacturers. *Women's Wear Daily,* 95.

Farameh, P. (Ed.) (2007). *Young fashion designers Americas.* Cologne, Germany: Daab.

Feitelberg, R. (2008, December 16). Vera to switch show locale. *Women's Wear Daily.* Retrieved January 8, 2009, from http://www.wwd.com/fashion-news/vera-to-switch-show-locale-1895622.
Finnane, A. (2008). *Changing clothes in China: Fashion, history, nation.* New York: Columbia University Press.
Fletcher, K. (2007). Clothes that connect. In Chapman, J., & Gant, N. (Eds.), *Designers, visionaries and other stories* (118–130). London: Earthscan.
Fletcher, K. (2008). *Sustainable fashion and textiles: Design journeys.* London: Earthscan.
Gobé, M. (2001). *Emotional branding.* New York: Allworth Press.
Golbin, P. (2001). *Fashion designers.* New York: Watson-Guptill.
Gonzalez, J. (2004). *Smart & interactive textiles: Advances in technology.* Retrieved March 16, 2009, from http://www.ualberta.ca/~jag3/smart_textiles/.
Griffiths, I. (2000). The invisible man. In White, N., & Griffiths, I. (Eds.), *The fashion business: Theory, practice, image* (69–90). Oxford: Berg.
Hauck, W. E. (2007). Cohort perception of luxury goods and services. *Journal of Fashion Marketing and Management,* 11(2), 175–188.
Hines, T. (2007). *Fashion marketing: Contemporary issues.* Oxford: Elsevier.
Hoffman, L. (Ed.) (2007). *Future fashion white papers.* New York: Earth Pledge.
Huckbody, J. (2003, August 1). Pierre Cardin, he's everywhere. *The Age.* Retrieved January 8, 2009, from http://www.theage.com.au/articles/2003/08/01/1059480531338.html.
Hume, M. (2009, April). Threads of change. *Time: Style & Design,* 32–35.
indiDenim. (n.d.). Retrieved March 14, 2009, from www.indidenim.com.
Johnson, C. (2004, December 15). "Smart" textiles emerge from nanotech labs: Garments may soon be communication devices. *CNBC.* Retrieved April 4, 2009, from http://www.msnbc.msn.com/id/6713188/.
Jones, R. M. (2006). *The apparel industry* (2nd ed.). West Sussex, UK: Blackwell.
Kaiser, A. (2008, April 25). Phillip Lim begins Japan push with Tokyo flagship. *Women's Wear Daily,* 3.
Karimzadeh, M. (2007, March 12). DVF takes tough stand against counterfeiters. *Women's Wear Daily,* 3.
Karimzadeh, M. (2008, March 24). As designer sales lag, retailers fret fashion in need of some fixing. *Women's Wear Daily,* 1.
Karra, N. (2008, December). The UK designer fashion economy. *NESTA.* Retrieved March 16, 2009, from http://www.nesta.org.uk/assets/Uploads/pdf/Policy-Briefing/designer_fashion_economy_policy_briefing_NESTA.pdf.
Kawamura, Y. (2004). *The Japanese revolution in Paris fashion.* Oxford: Berg.
Kawamura, Y. (2005). *Fashion-ology.* Oxford: Berg.
Keiser, S. J., & Garner, M.B.H. (2007). *Beyond design: The synergy of apparel product development* (2nd ed.). New York: Fairchild.
Kozel, S. (2008). Wearables: The flesh of social computing. In *Closer: Performance, technologies, phenomenology* (269–305). Cambridge, MA: MIT Press.
Lennon, C. (2009, April). The new gold standard. *Time: Style & Design,* 47–48.
Lillethun, S., & Welters, L. (2007). *The fashion reader.* Oxford: Berg.
Lipovetsky, G. (2002, July 1). *The empire of fashion: Dressing modern democracy.* Princeton, NJ: Princeton University Press.
Loker, S., Ashdown, S. P., Cowie, L., & Schoenfelder, K. A. (2004). Consumer interest in commercial applications of body scan data. *Journal of Textiles and Apparel, Management and Technology,* 4(1). http://www.tx.ncsu.edu/jtatm/.
Loker, S., Ashdown, S., & Schoenfelder, K. (2005). Size-specific analysis of body scan data to improve apparel fit. *Journal of Textile and Apparel, Management and Technology,* 4(3), 1–15.

McCann, J., & Bryson, D. (Eds.) (2009). *Smart clothes and wearable technology*. Cambridge, UK: Woodhead.

McNicoll, T. (2010, March 19). The fall of the house of Lacroix. *Newsweek*. Retrieved June 24, 2010, from http://www.newsweek.com/2010/03/18/the-fall-of-the-house-of-lacroix.html.

Medina, M. (2008, April 16). Von Furstenberg, Karan address luxe. *Women's Wear Daily*, 16.

Mendes, V. D., & DeLa Haye, A. (1999). *20th century fashion*. London: Thames & Hudson.

Menkes, S. (2009, March 25). Making a world of difference: Stella McCartney's style ethos. *New York Times*, 3. Retrieved April 21, 2009, from http://query.nytimes.com /gst/fullpage.html?res=9406E5DF143FF936A15750C0A96F9C8B63&sec=&spon=&pagewanted=1.

Mode à Paris. (n.d.). Retrieved November 20, 2008, from http://www.modeaparis. com/va/index.html.

Montero, G. (2008). A stitch in time: The history of New York's fashion district. *The Fashion Center*. Retrieved February 20, 2009, from http://www.fashioncenter.com/ history/index.html.

Naisbit, J. (2006). *Mind set! Reset your thinking and predict the future*. New York: Harper Collins.

Okonkwo, U. (2007). *Luxury fashion branding*. New York: Palgrave MacMillan.

O'Mahony, M., & Braddock, S. E. (2002). *Sportstech: Revolutionary fabrics, fashion, and design*. London: Thames & Hudson.

Pasquarelli, A. (2008, December, 23). Fashion week threatened by economy. *Crain's New York business.com*. Retrieved January 26, 2009, from http://www. crainsnewyork.com/article/20081223/FREE/812239982#.

Patner, J. (2004, September 13). Fashion week FAQ: Your nagging questions answered. *Slate*. Retrieved January 8, 2009, from http://www.slate.com/?id=2106639.

Pink, D. (2005). *A whole new mind*. New York: Penguin.

The Princeton Review. (n.d.). *Fashion designer*. Retrieved March 14, 2009, from http://www.princetonreview.com/careers.aspx?cid=63.

Quinn, B. (2002). *Techno fashion*. Oxford: Berg.

Rantisi, N. M. (2006). How New York stole modern fashion. In Breward, C., & Gilbert, D. (Eds.), *Fashion's world cities* (109–122). Oxford: Berg.

Rissanen, T. (2009). Creating fashion without the creation of fabric waste. In Hethorn, J., & Ulasewics, C. (Eds.), *Sustainable fashion: Why now? A conversation about issues, practices, and possibilities* (184–206). New York: Fairchild Books.

Root, R. A. (2005). *The Latin American fashion reader*. Oxford: Berg.

Seymour, S. (2008). *Fashionable technology: The intersection of design, fashion, science and technology*. New York: Springer.

Shields, R. (2008, August, 24). Brazilian style: South American fashion on the world stage. *The Independent*. Retrieved February 21, 2009, from http://www.independent.co.uk /life-style/fashion/news/brazilian-style-south-american-fashion-on-the-world-stage-907215.html.

Socha, M. (2007, June 1). Lights, camera, action: Showbiz moguls become fashion players. *Women's Wear Daily*, 1.

Socha, M. (2008, September 26). Q & A Suzy Menkes. *Women's Wear Daily*, 21.

Steele, V. (1988). *Paris fashion: A cultural history*. Oxford: Berg.

Steele, V. (1997). *Fifty years of fashion: From new look to now*. New Haven, CT: Yale University Press.

Steele, V., Mears, P., & Sauro, C. (2007). *Ralph Rucci: The art of weightlessness*. New Haven, CT: Yale University Press.

Stylios, G. (2004). An introduction to smart textiles. *International Journal of Clothing Science and Technology*, 16(5).

Sugimoto, Y. (n.d.). Fashion history of Japan. *Japan External Trade Organization*. Retrieved February 20, 2009, from http://www. jetro.org/trends/fashion_history_japan.php.

Tam, F. Y., Chan, T. S., Chu, P. W., & Wang, L. L. (2005). Opportunities and challenges: Hong Kong as Asia's fashion hub. *Journal of Fashion Marketing and Management*, 9(2), 221–231.
Thomas, D. (2007). *Deluxe: How luxury lost its luster.* London: Penguin Press.
Top fashion cities of 2008 named in annual survey. (2008, July 15). *The Global Language Monitor.* Retrieved January 12, 2009, from http://www.languagemonitor. com/fashion.
Trebay, G. (2008, September 4). Wanted: Genius designer. *New York Times.* Retrieved March 25, 2009, from http://www.nytimes.com/2008/09/04/fashion/shows/04fashion.html?pagewanted=1&_r=1.
Troy, T. J. (2003). *Couture culture: A study in modern art and fashion.* Cambridge, MA: MIT Press.
Tutton, M. (2008, October 27). Futuristic fashion gets smart. *CNN.* Retrieved March 16, 2009, from http://edition.cnn.com/2008/TECH/science/10/24/future.fashion/index.html.
United Nations. (1987). *Report of the world commission on environment and development,* General assembly resolution 42/187, 11 December 1987. Retrieved March 18, 2009, from http://www.un.org/documents/ga/res/42/ares42–187.htm.
von Furstenberg, D. (2007, August 24). Von Furstenberg: Fashion deserves copyright protection. *Los Angeles Times.* Retrieved January 8, 2009, from http://www.latimes.com/news/ opinion/la-oew-furstenberg24aug24,0,1109807.story.
Waddell, G. (2004). *How fashion works: Couture, ready-to-wear and mass production.* Oxford: Blackwell.
Wagner, A. (2008). The craft/ industry conundrum. *American Craft,* 68(2), 20.
Walker, S. (2006). *Sustainable by design: Explorations in theory and practice.* London: Earthscan.
Waters, R. (2005). *The trendmaster's guide: Get a jump on what your customer wants next.* New York: Penguin.
Welters, L., & Cunningham, P. (Eds.) (2005). *Twentieth-century American fashion.* Oxford: Berg.
White, N. (2000). *Reconstructing Italian fashion: America and the development of the Italian fashion industry.* Oxford: Berg.
White, N., & Griffiths, I. (2000). *The fashion business: Theory, practice, image.* Oxford: Berg.
Women's Wear Daily Staff. (2008, April 22). It's a small world: Fashion breaks down barriers around the globe. *Women's Wear Daily,* 1.
Women's Wear Daily Staff. (2009, April 13). The shifting paradigm: Rules being redefined for fashion and retail. *Women's Wear Daily,* 1.

INDEX